Teaching
Short Films

Symon Quy

Series Editor: Vivienne Clark
Commissioning Editor: Wendy Earle

British Library Cataloguing-in-Publication Data
A catalogue record for this guide is available from the British Library

ISBN 978 1 84457 1468

First published in 2007 by the British Film Institute
21 Stephen Street, London W1T 1LN

Student worksheets to support this guide are supplied at: www.bfi.org.uk/tfms
User name: **shorts@bfi.org.uk** Password: **te1203sf**

Design: Amanda Hawkes
Cover photographs: *About a Girl*, *Desserts*, *Two Cars, One Night*, *How They Got There*
(clockwise) courtesy of BFI Stills
Printed in Great Britain by: Cromwell Press Ltd

www.bfi.org.uk
There's more to discover about film and television through the BFI.
Our world-renowned archive, cinemas, festivals, films, publications
and learning resources are here to inspire you.

Contents

Introduction to the series

Since the introduction of the revised post-16 qualifications (AS and A2 Level) in the UK in September 2000, the number of students taking A Level Film and Media Studies has increased significantly, a trend shown by the latest entry statistics.

Subject & Level	June 2001	June 2002	June 2005	June 2006
A Level Film Studies+	2017	–	–	–
AS Level Film Studies	3852	–	9188	9703
A2 Level Film Studies	–	2175	4913	5898
A Level Media Studies*+	16,293	–	–	–
AS Level Media Studies*	22,872	–	32,346	33,542
A2 Level Media Studies*	–	18,150	23,427	25,192

*Three combined awarding bodies' results
+Legacy syllabus – last entry June 2001
(Source: BFI Education website – AS/A2 statistics refer to cashed-in entries only)

Furthermore, changes to the 14–19 curriculum currently in development for 2008 will doubtless see further increases in the take-up of courses (and indeed new courses) in this popular subject area. In response to this continuing expansion (unabated despite criticism from ill-informed pundits), a professional association of media educators in the UK (MEA – www.mediaedassociation.org.uk) has been formed to support teachers at all levels in all learning contexts, as well as to provide much-needed accurate public relations information and guidance about the many courses on offer and how to differentiate between them.

Inevitably these increases in student numbers have led to a pressing demand for more teachers and both new and experienced teachers (from other disciplines) alike may be faced with teaching these subjects for the first time, without necessarily a degree-level background to help them with subject content and conceptual understanding. In addition, frequently changing specifications see the arrival of new set topics and areas of study, so there is a continued need for up-to-date resources to aid teacher preparation. Media study is most effective when it responds to current media output and issues and it is the aim of this series to provide reference to recent media texts and products as well as to older ones.

I developed the concept and format of this series with the above factors, and busy and enthusiastic teachers and creative and energetic students, in mind. Each title provides an accessible reference resource, with essential topic content, as well as clear guidance on good classroom practice to improve the quality of teaching and students' learning. As well as supporting the teacher new to these subjects, the series provides the experienced specialist with new critical perspectives and teaching approaches as well as useful content.

The four sample schemes of work included in Section 1 are intended as practical models to help get teachers started. They are not prescriptive, as any effective scheme of work has to be developed with the specific requirements of an assessment context, and the ability of the teaching group, in mind. Likewise, the worksheets provided in the online materials offer examples of good practice, which can be adapted to specific needs and contexts. In some cases, the online provision includes additional resources, such as interviews and illustrative material, available as webnotes. See www.bfi.org.uk/tfms.

The series is clear evidence of the range, depth and breadth of teacher expertise and specialist knowledge required at A Level in these subjects. Also, it is an affirmation of why this subject area is such an important, rich and compelling one for increasing numbers of 16- to 19-year-old students. Many of the more theoretical titles in the series include reference to practical exercises involving media production skills. It is important that it is understood here that the current A Levels in Media and Film Studies are not designed as vocational, or pre-vocational, qualifications. In these contexts, the place of practical media production is to offer students active, creative and engaging ways in which to explore theory and reflect on their own practice.

It has been very gratifying to see that several titles in this series have found an international audience, in the USA, Canada and Australia, among other countries, and we hope that future titles continue to be of interest in international moving image education. Every author in the series is an experienced teacher of Film and/or Media Studies at this level and many have examining/moderating experience. It has been a pleasure to work so closely with such a diverse range of committed professionals and I should like to thank them for their individual contributions to this expanding series.

Vivienne Clark
Series Editor
February 2007

● Key features

- Assessment contexts for the major UK post-16 Film and Media Studies specifications
- Suggested schemes of work
- Historical contexts (where appropriate)
- Key facts, statistics and terms
- Detailed reference to the key concepts of Film and Media Studies
- Detailed case studies
- Glossaries
- Bibliographies
- Student worksheets, activities and resources (available online) – ready to print and photocopy for the classroom.

● Other titles in the series

- *Teaching Scriptwriting, Screenplays and Storyboards for Film and TV Production* (Mark Readman)
- *Teaching TV Sitcom* (James Baker)
- *Teaching Digital Video Production* (Pete Fraser and Barney Oram)
- *Teaching TV News* (Eileen Lewis)
- *Teaching Women and Film* (Sarah Gilligan)
- *Teaching World Cinema* (Kate Gamm)
- *Teaching TV Soaps* (Lou Alexander and Alison Cousens)
- *Teaching Contemporary British Broadcasting* (Rachel Viney)
- *Teaching Contemporary British Cinema* (Sarah Casey Benyahia)
- *Teaching Music Video* (Pete Fraser)
- *Teaching Auteur Study* (David Wharton and Jeremy Grant)
- *Teaching Analysis of Film Language* (David Wharton and Jeremy Grant)
- *Teaching Men and Film* (Matthew Hall)
- *Teaching Film Censorship and Controversy* (Mark Readman)
- *Teaching Stars and Performance* (Jill Poppy)
- *Teaching Video Games* (James Newman and Barney Oram)
- *Teaching Black Cinema* (Peter Jones)
- *Teaching Film and TV Documentary* (Sarah Casey Benyahia)
- *Teaching TV Drama* (Jeremy Points).

SERIES EDITOR: Vivienne Clark is a teacher of Film and Media Studies at Langley Park School for Boys, Beckenham, Kent and an Advanced Skills Teacher. She is an Associate Tutor of BFI Education and formerly a Principal Examiner for A Level Media Studies for one of the English awarding bodies. She is a freelance teacher trainer, media education consultant and writer/editor, with several published textbooks and resources, including *GCSE Media Studies* (Longman 2002), *Key Concepts and Skills for Media Studies*

(Hodder Arnold 2002) and *The Complete A-Z Film and Media Studies Handbook* (Hodder & Stoughton 2007). She is also a course tutor for the BFI/Institute of Education MA module, An Introduction to Media Education Practice.

AUTHOR: **Symon Quy** is Senior Lecturer in Media Education at the Central School of Speech and Drama, where he runs the Postgraduate Certificate of Education in Media Studies – training teachers in Media and Film as their specialist subject. He has taught Media Studies for 15 years in various secondary and further education contexts and examined A Level Film Studies. Symon is an Associate Tutor of the BFI and was the recipient of a Higher Education Academy National Teaching Fellowship in 2005.

1

Introduction

Assessment contexts

Awarding body & level	Subject	Unit code	Module/Topic
✓ AQA AS Level	Media Studies	MED1	Reading the Media
✓ AQA AS	Media Studies	MED3	Practical Production
✓ AQA A2	Media Studies	MED5	Independent Study
✓ Edexcel AS Communication and Production	Media	Unit 4	Make a Media Product
✓ Edexcel A2 Communication and Production	Media	Unit 10	Video Production and Editing Techniques
✓ Edexcel A2 Communication and Production	Media	Unit 17	Single Camera Drama Production
✓ OCR AS	Media Studies	2730	Foundation Production
✓ OCR A2	Media Studies	2733	Advanced Production
✓ WJEC AS	Film Studies	FS1	Making Meaning 1
✓ WJEC AS	Film Studies	FS4	Making Meaning 2
✓ WJEC AS	Media Studies	ME3	Making Media Texts
✓ WJEC A2	Media Studies	ME4	Investigating Media Texts
✓ CCEA AS	Moving Image Arts	AS2	Creative Production
✓ CCEA A2	Moving Image Arts	A2 1	Creative Production and Research
✓ SQA Higher	Media Studies	D334 12	Media Production
✓ SQA Advanced Higher	Media Studies	D334 13	Media Production
✓ SQA Higher	Media Literacy	D6TX 12	Film

• Specification links

The following specification links are possible through the study of short film as a broad, as well as a specialist, topic. This guide will help teachers following a specification with opportunities for the theoretical analysis of film and/or opportunities for practical production. Some specifications also offer opportunities to consider institutional processes such as the marketing and distribution of short film and this dimension will also serve students who are seeking a wider audience for their short films than just their course examiners.

AQA Media Studies – AS Module 3 Practical Production
Candidates have the opportunity to use one or more media technologies to produce a finished piece of practical coursework with accompanying written materials.

AQA Media Studies – A2 Module 5 Independent Study
Candidates can research in depth a contemporary media text (produced within the last two years) such as a short film or issues arising out of contemporary media texts such as institutional initiatives like the UK Film Council's Digital Shorts scheme.

Edexcel Media Communication and Production – AS Unit 4 Make a Media Product
Candidates can make a short film and present an accompanying portfolio of pre-production, production and post-production materials and an evaluation of the theoretical and creative processes of production.

Edexcel Media Communication and Production – A2 Unit 10 Video Production and Editing Techniques
This unit consolidates and develops practical production skills in short video production and editing. It emphasises a teamwork approach and the development of knowledge and understanding around different formats and key roles in an industrial context.

Edexcel Media Communication and Production – A2 Unit 17 Single Camera Drama Production
This unit requires students to plan and produce a short drama that has been developed from research into differing programme styles and production contexts. The exercise is conceived to explore the codes and conventions of current industrial practice.

OCR Media Studies – AS Unit 2730 Foundation Production
Candidates need to demonstrate a range of technical skills and understanding of media concepts by constructing their own media text. The set briefs in film and television can be effectively supported by an exploration and analysis of the short film form.

OCR Media Studies – A2 Unit 2733 Advanced Production

This unit builds on the knowledge, understanding and skills already acquired and requires candidates to create 'a short film, in its entirety of maximum five minutes duration'. There are collaborative and individual elements to each unit of assessment on the OCR specifications.

CCEA Moving Image Arts – AS Unit AS2 Creative Production

Students need to develop for submission the pre-production materials (synopsis, script, storyboard, shot list and shooting schedule) for a media product (such as a short film) between three and five minutes in length.

CCEA Moving Image Arts – A2 Unit A2 1 Creative Production and Research

Students need to prepare and produce a text – between five and seven minutes long – 'constituting a complete narrative film in its own right', with an accompanying written evaluation making reasoned judgments on the formal and stylistic outcomes of the production.

WJEC Film Studies – AS Unit FS1 Making Meaning 1

Learning in this unit focuses on film form and the production of meaning. The unit is assessed through the written study of (1) genres and narrative (2) film language – image composition, cinematography, editing and sound. The practical application of this learning is expressed in the production of a synopsis, screenplay extract and storyboard/photoboard.

WJEC Film Studies – AS Unit FS4 Making Meaning 2

The practical production element of this unit requires candidates to produce a synopsis and a complete short film of between three and five minutes in length, either individually or in groups of no more than four. The specification guidance suggests a division of production roles into four areas: direction, cinematography, editing and sound.

WJEC Media Studies – AS Unit ME3 Making Media Texts

This unit is designed to enable candidates to show their knowledge and understanding of media practice through their engagement with the planning, processing and evaluation stages of media productions. The assessment requirements comprise a portfolio of two elements from the pre-production process (such as a script and storyboard) and one short production of up to three minutes in length.

WJEC Media Studies – A2 Unit ME4 Investigating Media Texts

This unit is conceived as an evaluative and investigative opportunity to explore an area of media output in depth. Candidates are required to compare two media texts (such as short films) in an essay of 2,000–3,000 words.

SQA Media Studies – Higher Unit D334 12 Media Production

The principle underlying this unit is that the candidates gain a knowledge and understanding of the processes of media production. The specifications advocate groups of, typically, six students who work collaboratively to produce a short film or animation of 5 to 10 minutes in length.

SQA Media Studies – Advanced Higher Unit D334 13 Media Production

This unit is designed to enable candidates to contribute to all stages of media production, such as a short film of 5 to 10 minutes' duration. Though production work is likely to be of a collaborative nature, the reporting and evaluation of the product is individual.

SQA Media Literacy – Higher Unit D6TX 12 Film

This unit is designed to enable the candidate to analyse film language, study the effects of film as industry on film as art, consider the relationship between the cinema audience and film and apply understanding of the concepts of narrative and representation to film analysis. Given *Scottish Screen's* patronage of short films, these areas can readily be approached through an investigation of Scottish national cinema.

Further resources to support learning and teaching

The following titles in this series would also be useful companions to this pack:
- *Teaching Analysis of Film Language* David Wharton and Jeremy Grant – for a full exploration of film language and how to analyse films.
- *Teaching Scriptwriting, Screenplays and Storyboards for Film and TV Production* Mark Readman – for pre-production methodologies in the planning stage of short filmmaking.
- *Teaching Digital Video Production* Pete Fraser and Barney Oram – for practical and theoretical guidance on using digital technologies to create films.

In addition the BFI publishes a range of short film compilations including
- *Moving Shorts* – short live-action and animation films covering a range of themes and film styles.
- *Real Shorts* – non-fiction films from 3 to18 minutes long, including films from the beginning of the 20th century.

Each compilation is supported online by downloadable teaching guidelines, film-related materials and student worksheets. See www.bfi.org.uk/teaching/secondary.

What is short film?

How should we best make sense of the term 'short film'? It will be helpful to reach shared understandings with your students in considering short film's various constituent qualities. Your classes will benefit from being led towards a definition that recognises the complexities behind what might otherwise be considered to be a straightforward and unproblematic term. To work towards a definition and understanding of the short film with your students, see **Worksheet 1**.

worksheet ① **Thinking about short films**

1 How would you define the term 'short film'? Write a definition of the term for an online encyclopaedia.
2 What are your expectations of a text that is described as a 'short film'?
3 Where might you expect to be able to view short films?
4 If we consider Catherine Des Forges' notion that short films comprise 'spare, economic narrative, interesting storytelling; well-structured work which draws in the audience quickly', how many different types of media texts can be described as short film? Please add to the following list: cartoons, music videos, video diaries, documentaries ...
5 Short films are often compared (usually negatively) with popular feature-length films. Apart from their length, how do short films differ from feature-length films? Complete the grid below, which draws comparisons between our expectations of these film forms. The first few have been done for you:

Feature-length film	Short film
Around 100 minutes	Around 10 minutes
Big budget	Low budget
Professional	Amateur
Mainstream	Alternative
Formulaic	Experimental
Widely distributed	Rarely screened
Mass audience	Niche audience
Large casts	Small casts
Glossy	Grainy

Page 1 of 2   Short Films

1 of 2 pages

To access student worksheets and other online materials go to *Teaching Short Films* at **www.bfi.org.uk/tfms** and enter User name: **shorts@bfi.org.uk** and Password: **te1203sf**.

● Defined by length?

Though the term 'short film' might be applied to any film of less than standard feature film duration (90–120 minutes), a consensus is emerging within the industry at the start of the 21st century that a short should be no longer than 40 minutes. The Academy of Motion Picture Arts and Sciences awards its Oscars™ to short films of up to this length. Gareth Evans in *In Short: A Guide to Short Film-making in the Digital Age* (Elsey and Kelly, 2002, p xi) suggests that 'short films are long films that finish earlier'; indicating that such films need to imply more than they can show in their limited screen time. However, substantially briefer films, some of no more than five minutes, are also established in the sector; these are dubbed 'micro shorts'. Online web-cinemas are able to showcase such short films in digital formats. Cobravision provides a typical example of the experimentation with the length of the short film form: these are merely five seconds in duration. However, in the context of modern education, most awarding bodies require students to make films of no more than five minutes length in their practical units.

● Defined by content?

Short fiction films might be considered as the literary equivalent of the poem or short story, if the feature film has come to represent the novel. The best short films are, according to Gareth Evans, 'crystalline creations of precise, prismatic intensity'. Short film is 'a good idea, succinctly told. Less is more,' says Dave Sproxton of Aardman Animations. Such definitions are indicative of the form's (quint)essential quality: they are the effective realisation of one particular idea. This might be, for instance, through the depiction of a carefully considered emotion or the capture of a particular moment. Good short films represent a refinement of ideas and the distilled essences of their creators' imaginations.

● Defined by form?

As far as the content of short films is concerned, there is the same variety and diversity that their longer-length counterparts provide. Short films can be fiction or non-fiction, and might be individual enterprises or collaborative endeavours. Ultimately, the forms and functions of the short film should be recognised as multifarious. The flexibility of the short film is perhaps its greatest asset; it crosses the boundaries of all categories of film production, as is manifest in films of quality in the forms of propaganda, advertising, documentary, music video, animation and *avant garde* film.

● Defined as vocational?

Short film production has long been a laboratory for experimentation and innovation. For many of those who have worked on successful short films, their 'visions of light' have been a passport to the vocations associated with feature-length production work. Short films are often included on the showreel portfolios that are considered to be an apprenticeship for professional filmmaking. The term 'calling card' film has been used to describe those short films that seek to establish the identity of their creators and get them a foot in the door of the business. In essence, the UK Film Council's various short film initiatives seek to serve this purpose; supporting budget filmmaking with the hope of improving the national cinema industry.

● Defined by means of production?

For the purposes of this guide, the term 'short film' is an inclusive one that refers to all short sequences of moving images – whether shot for exhibition through television, cinema or other media, such as personal computers and mobile phones. Furthermore, short film in this definition might be produced by the use of a diverse range of technologies rather than being shot purely on film stock.

● Defined as 'other'?

Short film is frequently talked about in terms of what it is not. For instance, it is frequently (and unfairly) compared with the dominant form of the feature-length film. Short film has long been associated with alternative filmmaking, both in terms of its content and the freedom of expression it affords. Away from the constraints of industrial production, high finance and the need to tailor films to the expectations of audiences, those who make short films are more likely to retain creative control.

Rationale: Why teach short film?

There are very good reasons for studying short film, beyond the assessment requirements of various examinations.

● To widen students' experiences of the short film form

Our students' experience of cinema is likely to be quite narrow. Students are unlikely to have seen the range of short films now available to teachers, either from conventional sources such as television broadcasts, or through the new media that are emerging at the start of the 21st century, such as web cinemas.

Fact sheet: Short films by decade provides a list of key short film directors that students might add to as their work develops.

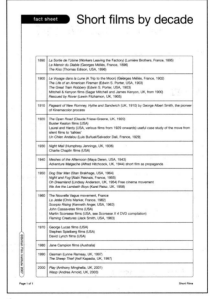

1 page

● To address time constraints

Short films use the same modes of communication as their longer-length counterparts and provide similar opportunities for textual analysis. In the time-pressured environments of contemporary classrooms, using short films allows students to see entire texts rather than the extracts of feature-length texts that teachers have become accustomed to using. Analytical approaches to the study of film, for instance, those related to narrative structure or representation theories, can be considered through short film with as much success as through feature films.

● To take advantage of the recently enhanced availability of short films

The availability of films themselves has increased considerably in recent years. The 10-minute short film has been a major focus for public funding in the UK for over 10 years, with short film strands like the BBC's 10x10 and Brief Encounters; Channel 4's Short and Curlies, the British Film Institute's New Directors programme and the Film Council's Digital Shorts. The proliferation of cable channels has created opportunities for the short film to find additional places in modern programme schedules. Film 4, for instance, now gives regular slots to short films in its Shooting Gallery series and offers a back catalogue through the 'shorts & clips' page on its website. In exhibition terms, short film seems to have found places that it was previously denied. There is a growing number of regularly scheduled short film showcase screenings at regional cinemas, such as Future Shorts and the First Run series at Picturehouse cinemas.

● To recognise how media companies and institutions are targeting new audiences through emerging technologies and how media forms are converging

This trend is set to continue: as media forms diverge (and home computers become television screens), broadcasting becomes narrowcasting and marketing focuses on reaching niche audiences. Finding new markets and access to emerging audiences is an ongoing challenge for the film industry. The new generation of 3G mobile phones is a good example of technology supporting innovative practice. Handsets now have the capacity to provide a new medium for the production and exhibition of digitalised short films to fee-paying audiences, with each film priced on a pay-per-download basis.

● To maintain the topicality of our teaching

Short films have recently become a marketable commodity in their own right, in terms of domestic consumption. The availability of many films on DVD is one key resource issue in itself that is worth discussing with students. Smaller distributors in the more advanced economies of the world are now taking advantage of DVD technology by releasing a wider range of titles for commercial sale (such as the *Cinema 16* series) or as give-aways with magazines and newspapers (such as *Sight and Sound* and *The Times'* *FilmFirst* promotions). Websites that allow customers to choose short films from extensive back catalogues now provide an outlet for the sale of short films. For instance, www.customflix.com charges to copy up to 10 short films onto a DVD and sends it through the post to customers.

● To provide students with insights into various production contexts

Understanding the place of short film within the film industry, allows students to go some way towards understanding the ways in which the industry operates as a whole. Lewis' *How to Make Great Short Feature Films: The*

Making of Ghosthunter (2001) is a book and Channel 4 documentary. It provides insights into the various roles required in short film production, such as sound engineering and direction, as well as a DVD-ROM of production paperwork.

- To develop students' appreciation of historical and institutional modes of production

Studying the history of short film is, of course, investigating the development of the medium itself. The relationship between short films and feature films is a multi dimensional and complex one. Where the feature-length film has tended to dominate the marketplace and critical appreciation, the short film has been seen as the agent of change and experimentation. In the Golden Age of the Hollywood studio system, in the 1930s, the studios would have production teams making short films and B-movies on lots that were essentially the training ground for makers of feature films. This mode of production eventually became cost-prohibitive and the independent sector took up the challenge in providing the laboratory for experimental film production, making short films with full creative control.

- To demystify the processes of production, distribution and exhibition

Studying short film is a way in to exploring the current state of the global industry of film production and national cinemas. Patterns of ownership and finance in different countries can be compared with types of production and cultural, ideological and economic perspectives. If Hollywood has been identified as the institution *par excellence* for the manufacture and distribution of the mainstream feature-length film, then how have other countries countered this in the production of short films with different intentions and under different circumstances? Tracing the production and exhibition of a successful short film through its various stages will provide students with insights into the processes behind the product. The 'Depict! 90 second film festival' teaching resources for Rachel Tillotson's prize-winning film *As I Was Falling* provide a model for such an investigation (www.depict.org/content/education).

- To better facilitate practical production work and empower learners in and out of the classroom

As practical work has developed in examination specifications, so has the need for an approach that integrates theoretical ideas with opportunities for their creative application. Short film is ideal as a means of exploring the relationships between the processes and the products of filmmaking. Prohibitively expensive technical equipment is no longer an obstacle to young people who are increasingly able to get their hands on the means of production (in both senses of the phrase). The variety of formats has never been greater. Where previously, the formats of Super 8 or 16mm required certain specialist skills and knowledge, considered by many to be beyond the reach of schools, the home-computer boom has provided an integrated workstation for the manufacture and exhibition of short films that is no longer the preserve of the specialist.

- To provide students with opportunities to develop vocational skills and enter the film industry

It has long been understood that short films provide a very limited number of filmmakers with a passport to the industry. Filmmakers such as George Lucas, Francis Ford Coppola, Martin Scorsese, Roman Polanski, Jim Jarmusch and Spike Lee all started their careers by making 'calling card shorts'. Jarmusch later returned to the form in his portmanteau feature *Coffee and Cigarettes* (US, 2003) (a feature-length combination of thematically linked short films).

- To celebrate a neglected art form

Certainly, it is high time that short films were considered an art form in their own right and exploited for their untapped potential in both commercial and educational terms.

How to use this guide

This guide provides an introduction to methods and case studies to support the teaching of short film to Media and Film students in a range of assessment contexts. The overarching intention is to enable you to teach the topic, using both the conceptual frameworks of Film and Media Studies and a set of varied examples of short films. The guide sets out to develop students' understanding of effective processes in short film production. Learners are taken through the various stages 'from script to screen' to produce finished products that are creatively informed as well as critically engaged.

The key aims of this guide are:
- To promote the use of short film as an educationally valuable and underutilised form of film as art and film as industry.
- To provide frameworks for studying short films and suggest a conceptual approach to the analysis of texts (moving image language; genre; representation; audience; narratives; institutions; technologies).
- To provide a selected history of the short film in its various manifestations: from primitive cinema to the digital age.
- To encourage teachers to explore the rich material found in short film and look for opportunities to use such films in the classroom more frequently.
- To provide guidance for teachers and students involved in the practical production of short films.
- To consider vocational issues and to suggest ways forward in the marketing and exhibition of short films.

The schemes of work that follow establish a series of approaches to teaching short films that are revisited and reinforced by the activities and case studies. The schemes of work provide guidelines, but you will need to amend them to meet the needs of your learners and your own pedagogy.

Section 1 of this guide has outlined a variety of examination specifications, detailing units in which the analysis and practical production of short films might be appropriate. Four schemes of work are also suggested. Scheme of work 1 establishes how short films communicate with audiences through moving image language. Scheme of work 2 investigates moving image key concepts, while Scheme of work 3 investigates institutional and vocational dimensions. Scheme of work 4 focuses on issues in the practical production of short films within Media Studies courses and offers ways forward for the busy teaching professional. Section 2 seeks to establish a body of knowledge and understanding of the background to the short film form through a timeline and examines the history of the form's development. It also investigates the new opportunities for short film production and distribution in the digital age. Section 3 provides three detailed case studies that are aligned with the topics explored in each of the first three schemes of work.

This guide necessarily deals mostly with promoting a conceptual approach to the analysis and production of short film. Towards its end, however, are suggestions for books and resources that support the teaching and learning of film criticism and production that can be used in conjunction with this guide. The sub sections that follow the Glossary have been constructed so that they might easily form worksheets to be distributed to learners as study aids. This guide is supported by a variety of online resources that provide further information and case studies, together with worksheets that encourage students to reflect upon their own consumption of film, develop skills in textual analysis and practical production and to undertake independent research.

The worksheets to support these exercises are available at www.bfi.org.uk/tfms. To access the pages, enter username: **shorts** and the password: **te1203sh**. If you have any problems, email: educationresources@bfi.org.uk.

Getting started

A useful starting point is for students to formulate or challenge ideas about what the term 'short film' might mean and to consider the vast range of media texts and products that fall under the umbrella of the term 'short film'. (See **Worksheet 1**) Learners should go on to compare the forms and functions of short films with their feature-length counterparts. Students should then be encouraged to consider their own patterns of consumption of these different types of film and how contrasting audiences use of short film.

Having considered definitions of short film and their forms and functions, students should undertake some internet research into the distribution and exhibition of short films. Their findings should reveal a wider perspective on the profile of short films, including awards and nominations at film festivals. Students should learn how short film production and exhibition is positioned in comparison to feature-length films.

● Sourcing short films for the classroom

A key consideration in writing this guide was the accessibility of short films. To a great extent this has guided the choice of films. The case study films aside, all other suggestions can be replaced by suitable general alternatives. Purchasing several of the commercially available compilation DVDs from the following list is likely to prove a sound investment in quality terms. Luke Morris, the 'curator' of the *Cinema 16* compilations and a short filmmaker himself recognises that short film compilations are a new market. *'When you think of the number of young short-filmmakers working today, there's a captive audience that wants to analyse these films.'* The first *Cinema 16 – British Short Films* DVD sold more than 5,000 copies in the UK in the first year of its release, which is more than a typical foreign-language feature would be expected to sell over the same period.

BFI short film DVD compilations with online resources – produced for schools and colleges:
- *Screening Shorts*
- *Moving Shorts*
- *Real Shorts*

A selection of other BFI short film DVDs:
- *Early Cinema: Primitives and Pioneers*
- *Free Cinema*
- *Un Chien Andalou and L'Age D'Or*
- *Geoffrey Jones: The Rhythm of Film*
- *The Early Films of Peter Greenaway*

English and Media Centre publications:
- *Key Stage 3 Media Book* and accompanying DVD
- *Key Stage 4 Media Pack* and accompanying DVD
- *Double Take* short film pack

Film Education DVD compilation with interactive resources:
- *MoPix ScreenStory*

Short film DVD Compilations:
- *Cinema 16 – British Short Films; European Short Films; American Short Films*

- *Best v Best* – Vol One and Vol Two
- *Best of Resfest* – Vols 1–3
- Onedotzero DVDs – Vols 1–4
- *Director's Label* series releases
- *Raindance Film Festival Shorts* – annual DVD
- Future Shorts DVDs (single short film releases)
- *Lumière & Company*
- *11'09"01 – September 11*
- *The Reel* (the advertising industry's monthly DVD showcase that goes out to 1200 advertising agencies and over 600 production companies).
- *Res* magazine (a bi monthly publication with a free compilation DVD)

Other:
- Off-air recordings of Film 4 daily broadcasts provide high-quality productions
- There are more and more websites streaming short films – a selection is listed in the References and resources section.

Schemes of work

● Scheme of work 1: Short film and moving image language

Possible awarding body focus: WJEC Film Studies AS level (Unit FS1)
Time: Five weeks (four hours per week)

This unit has been designed to introduce students to concepts relating to the semiotics of film (the study of sign systems and meaning). It considers the aesthetics of sound and image in film. The initial focus film *About a Girl* (Brian Percival, UK, 2001) from the BFI's *Moving Shorts* or the *Cinema 16 – British Short Films* DVD compilation, is compared and contrasted with other short films.

Aims:
On completing this unit, students should be able to:
- Understand how film images are constructed through the use of *mise en scène*, cinematography, sound and editing in *About a Girl*
- Explain how these elements create meanings in specific scenes
- Apply these concepts to other short films

Outcomes:
- Students will acquire skills of close textual analysis (micro analysis) that can be used in any aspect of Media and Film Studies
- A coursework essay comparing and contrasting *About a Girl* with another short film

Week 1 Introduction to short films
Brainstorm the term 'short film'.
Discuss: What are students' expectations of short films?
Identify famous short film directors **Fact sheet**
Screening: microshort films (films less than 90 seconds in length)
Thinking about short films **Worksheet 1**
Textual Analysis of short films **Worksheet 2**
Screening: *About a Girl*
Consider student responses to the film

Week 2 Micro analysis of short film
Viewing notes 1 *About a Girl*
Introduction to moving image language – how film texts make meaning through signs
Mise en scène **Worksheet 3**
Reading film stills from *About a Girl*
About the Male photo shoot of a teen story **Worksheet 4**
Screening: *Visions of Light* (Arnold Glassman, US, 1992)
Cinematography **Worksheet 5**
Screening: *About a Girl* with director's commentary

Week 3 Sound
Consideration of sound choices in *About a Girl* **Worksheet 6**
Voiceover narration
Live-action dialogue
Synchronous/non-synchronous sound
Music/soundtrack
Screening: *How They Got There* (Spike Jonze with Mark Gonzales, USA, 1997) from the *Director's Label* compilation DVD
Viewing notes 2 *How They Got There*
Analysis of *How They Got There*

Week 4 Editing and special effects
About a Girl editing
Editing focus – editing choices and terminology **Worksheet 7**
Screening: *The Bypass* (Amit Kumar, UK, 2003)
Viewing notes 3
Analysis of editing choices in The *Bypass*

Week 5 Coursework
Group presentations of textual analysis of other short films
Worksheet 8
Students work on individual micro analysis of a short film of their own choice
Structuring an analytical essay **Worksheet 9**

● Scheme of work 2: Short film and key concepts

This unit will cover the following key concepts:
● Narrative
● Genre
● Representation
● Audience

This unit has been structured as a five-week block to address key issues of film appreciation and spectatorship and to consider how particular social groups, ideas and ideologies are represented on screen. The initial focus film *Two Cars, One Night* (Taika Waititi, New Zealand, 2003) (from the BFI's *Moving Shorts* DVD or the *Best v Best* Vol One DVD) is compared and contrasted with other short films.

Aims:
On completing this unit, students should be able to:
● Analyse short films holistically in relation to key film concepts and theory
● Explain how these aspects combine to create meanings in specific short films
● Apply these conceptual and theoretical aspects of film theory to other short films

Outcomes:
● Students will acquire skills of textual analysis (macro-analysis) that can be used in any aspect of Media and Film Studies
● Students will produce a research project and PowerPoint presentation on aspects of their chosen short films from Scheme of work 1

Week 1 Narrative and characterisation
Screening of *Two Cars, One Night*
Viewing notes 4
Screening of *Dad's Dead* (Chris Shepherd, UK, 2002) from the Onedotzero Volume 2 DVD
Screening: *The Making of Dad's Dead*
Screening: *Gasman* (Lynne Ramsay, UK, 1997) from the *Cinema 16 – British Short Films* DVD
Distribution of Lynne Ramsay interview in Elsey and Kelly *In Short: A Guide to Short Film-making in the Digital Age* (2002)
Worksheet 10 on narratives and plotlines

Week 2 Genre
Many short films work against genre categorisation or play with the conventions of generic forms. Investigate the various generic forms of the short film.
Screening: the drama *Helicopter* (Ari Gold, USA, 2000) from *Best of Resfest* Volume 2 DVD
Screening: the spoof documentary *Delusions in Modern Primitivism* (Daniel Loflin, USA, 2000) from *Best of Resfest* Volume 2 DVD
Worksheet 11 genre, codes and conventions

Week 3 Representation
Screening: *The Light of Darkness* (Michael Cargile, USA, 1998) from the *American Short Shorts 2000* DVD or available as an extra on the feature film DVD *Lay It Down* (Michael Cargile, USA, 2001)
Screening: *The Lunch Date* (Adam Davidson, USA, 1991) available on the Cinema 16 USA compilation DVD
Worksheet 12 on representation

Week 4 Audience
Screening: *As I Was Falling* (Rachel Tillotson, UK, 1999) Depict! website www.depict.org
This internet resource looks closely at *As I Was Falling*, the 60-second microfilm that won the Brief Encounters Depict! prize in 1999. It takes this film as a case study, and through interviews with its maker, Rachel Tillotson, examines the context in which the film was made and the filmmaker's working method. The site also provides information for new filmmakers about funding and the opportunities offered by festivals. For students of AS Level Film and GNVQ and Media Studies, there are a wide range of tasks, and suggestions for further reading.

Week 5 Coursework
Group presentations of textual analysis of other short films
Worksheet 8
Students work on individual macro analysis of a short film of their own choice
Structuring an analytical essay **Worksheet 9**

● Scheme of work 3: Research into the short film industry

Possible awarding body focus: OCR A2 Media Studies Advanced Production unit
Time: Five weeks (four hours per week)

This unit presents students with opportunities to explore the institutional contexts of short film production in regional, national and international contexts. Students are able to investigate the artists, companies and organisations that produce, promote and screen short films through individual research projects based on short films of their choice. A number of the worksheets in this scheme have been written with the flexible purpose of teaching students how to actually distribute and promote their own short films to festivals, competitions and online audiences, should they undertake the practical work of Scheme of work 4.

This scheme of work covers the following:
- Institutions
- Development
- Commissions
- Production
- Emerging technologies
- Production
- Distribution and exhibition
- Marketing
- Vocations

Aims:
On completing this unit, students should be able to:
- Understand how short films are successfully promoted and marketed to real audiences
- Actively market and promote their own short films

Outcomes:
- Individual research projects on chosen short films
- Students will collaborate to produce a marketing and promotion folder for their short films

Week 1 Researching the field
General overview of the short film industry **Worksheet 13**
Read 'In Short Supply' and discuss the form and function of short films in the digital age **Worksheet 14**
Consider marketing possibilities for single short film releases **Worksheet 15**
Explore the types of companies that operate in the short film industry **Worksheet 16**
Consider an online case study of the British Council organisation, *Britfilms*, which offers advice and guidance on short film marketing and promotions
Group work to investigate case studies of successful short films

Week 2 Emerging technologies/institutions/convergence
Investigate the BBC Film Network website
Explore Film 4 broadcast schedule for short films
Investigate Orange G3 downloads of short films to computers and mobile phones
Plan business presentation to company, activities developed in consultation with professional organisation 'Shooting People/Apple Education'
Research the distribution and exhibition of short films with 'search engine cinema' **Worksheet 17**

Week 3 Short film festivals and competitions
Raindance/Brief Encounters/Darklight/Ffresh (student film festival)/ competition case studies. Festivals and competitions in the References and resources section.
Internet research on festivals and competitions
Explore short film festivals **Worksheet 18**
Screening: *How to Submit Your Short Film to the Academy* – extra feature on the 75th Annual Academy Awards short films DVD (Questar entertainment)
Artistic property and the rights to your short film/gaining clearance
Investigate sponsorship of short film productions and festivals online
Programme a short film festival **Worksheet 19**

Week 4 Marketing short films
Plan a season of themed short films for Shooting Gallery on Film 4 **Worksheet 20**
Discuss the article 'Getting Your Short Film Shown' **Worksheet 21**
Produce packaging and promotional materials
Covers and blurbs, sleeve notes, press releases
Develop a media pack for your short film
Submit your short film to a web cinema **Worksheet 22**
Write a press release for your short film **Worksheet 23**

Week 5 Coursework
PowerPoint presentations of research into chosen short films

● Scheme of work 4: Short film practical production

Possible awarding body focus: OCR A2 Media Studies Advanced Production unit
Time: Five weeks (four hours per week)

This scheme has been conceived as an opportunity to extend the theoretical issues from the study of short film covered in Schemes 1, 2 and 3 into the practical production context. It is structured around the three-tiered production process by which short and feature-length films are most commonly produced. Although the scheme suggested is for a microshort, it can be extended for longer films. It follows the production practices for live-action, location-based filmmaking but could be amended to meet the needs of documentary or animation production.

Aims:

On completing this unit, students will have developed their knowledge and understanding of the three-tiered production process:

- Pre-production: synopsis, pitching a treatment, budgeting, script development, division of roles, casting and rehearsal, scheduling, storyboard/photoboard of locations
- Production: cast and crew codes of conduct, lighting, props, wardrobe, recording sound and images
- Post-production: editing, marketing, test screening

Outcomes:

- Students will collaborate to produce a short film and presentation on the process of film production
- Students will produce a production folder that evidences the three-tiered production process

Week 1   Introduce the three-tiered production process
Film production brief / Creating a production company **Worksheet 24a**
Screening: *Living in Oblivion* (Tom DiCillo, USA, 1995) – feature film
Production roles **Worksheet 24b**

Week 2   Pre-production
Screening: *Making It! As I was Falling* at www.depict.org.uk
Screening: *How to Make Great Short Feature Films: The Making of Ghosthunter* – DVD (and book)
Short film development – planning the stages **Worksheet 24c**
Writing short films **Worksheet 24d**
Pitching ideas – screen some of the Orange 'filmpitch' advertisements with John Cleese, Patrick Swayze, etc, or an early sequence of *The Player* (Robert Altman, USA, 1992)
Sceening: *The Pitch* (Doug Ellin, USA, 1993) for a 'How not to pitch' short film, starring David Schwimmer
Writing a synopsis **Worksheet 25**
Budgeting – time and finance
Cast and crew of production
Screening: *Ten Minutes* (Ben Mole, UK, 2002) and associated documentaries on filmmaking – Raindance 21-minute film school at ww.raindancefilmfestival.org

Screening: *Raindance Festival* 2004 DVD
Develop a treatment

Week 3 Pre-production
Scout locations – photograph likely venues and seek permission to film
Character profiles **Worksheet 26**
Camera exercises **Worksheet 27**
Script finalisation
Story photoboard
Rehearsals
Test shooting

Week 4 Production
Shooting and sound recording
Eliciting strong performances **Worksheet 28**
Production code of practice **Worksheet 29**
Scheduling and preparing call sheets **Worksheet 30**
View rushes
Rough-cut screening/test audience feedback

Week 5 Post-production
Log of accompanying materials
Edit trailer your short film: 'The making of ...'
Re-cut short film and positioning packaging and promotional materials to meet the entrance requirements of a range of festivals and competitions
Revisit 'Getting Your Short Film Shown' article **Worksheet 21**

Week 6 Screenings and presentations
Analysing aspects of the production **Worksheet 31**
Review writing
Final evaluations **Worksheet 32**
Glossary

2

Background

Timeline

A summary of key individuals and events in the film industry and the development of the short film (see also fact sheet 'Short films by decade'):

1895   *Sortie d'Usine (Workers Leaving the Factory)* (Lumière Brothers, France) – this is considered to be the first projected film. Auguste and Louis Lumière are credited with the world's first public film screening on 28 December 1895. Approximately 10 short films, lasting only 20 minutes in total, were shown in the basement lounge of the Grand Café on the Boulevard des Capucines in Paris. It was the very first public demonstration of the device they called the cinematographe, which effectively functioned as camera, projector and printer all in one.

1896   *The Kiss* (Thomas Edison, USA) – two people kiss. A single action as narrative; sex comes to the cinema; demands for censorship. A marker on the road to the social controversy about films – how films make meaning and what meanings they make.

1896   *Le Manoir du Diable* (Georges Méliès, France) – this silent short film was the first horror movie and the first vampire film.

1901   Mitchell and Kenyon make their documentaries of public events and industrial England from their Blackburn, Lancashire-based company.

1902   *Le Voyage dans la Lune* (A Trip to the Moon) (Georges Méliès, France) – this 14-minute version of the Jules Verne story is the screen's first sortie into science fiction.

1903   *The Great Train Robbery* (Edwin S Porter, USA) – if not the first narrative film, then the first film where the narrative was understood as storytelling.

1903   *The Life of an American Fireman* (Edwin S Porter, USA) – this film was influential in developing the grammar or language of film as we understand it today.

1905   *Rescued by Rover* (Lewin Fitzhamon, CM Hepworth, UK) – now considered to be a classic of early storytelling in film.
This film, along with many other examples of early cinema, can be viewed free online at www.screenonline.org.uk/education/student/primitives.

1910   *Pageant of New Romney, Hythe and Sandwich* (George Albert Smith, UK, pioneer of kinemacolour technique).

1927   The Academy of Motion Picture Arts and Sciences (AMPAS) is founded on 11 May 1927 in California to advance the arts and sciences of motion pictures. AMPAS later rules that a film short should be less than 40 minutes.

1928   *Steamboat Willie* (Ub Iwerks, USA) – the first in Walt Disney's Mickey Mouse series and the first successful sound cartoon animation.

1929   *Un Chien Andalou* (*An Andalusian Dog*) (France) – Luis Buñuel's infamous collaboration with Salvador Dali resulted in the archetypal experimental/*avant garde* short film.

1930   AMPAS establishes the 'Short Subjects Cartoons' category. This title is changed in 1971 to 'Short subjects animated films' to elevate the status of the form and include other forms of animation.

1932   The initiation by AMPAS of short subject awards for 1932–5. The categories established were 'Short Subjects, comedy' and 'Short Subjects, novelty'. The current title for this category, 'Live Action Short Film', was introduced in 1974. For the three preceding years it was known as 'Short Subjects, Live Action Films'. The term 'Short Subjects, Live Action Subjects' was used from 1957–70. From 1936–56 there were two separate awards, 'Short Subjects, one-reel' and 'Short Subjects, two-reel'. A third category 'Short Subjects, color' was used only in 1936 and 1937.

1933   Foundation of the British Film Institute (BFI) – a state-funded body charged with the mission to encourage the development of film culture.

1933   *Zéro de Conduite* (*Zero for Conduct*, France) – Jean Vigo's 41 minute long film tells a story of life in a boarding school in a poetic way.

1941   AMPAS establishes the 'Documentary Short Subject' category.

1942   *The Battle of Midway* (USA) – John Ford filmed this US Navy documentary of the Japanese attack on Midway. A powerful piece of wartime filmmaking.

1943   *Meshes of the Afternoon* (USA) – Maya Deren's dreamlike personal *avant-garde* film employs evocative and arresting imagery.

1955   *Night and Fog* (*Nuit et Bruillard*) (France) – Alain Resnais' documentary contrasts the tranquility of a desolate post-Holocaust concentration camp with the horrific events that occurred there during World War II.

1956	First screening of Free Cinema short films at the *National Film Theatre* in London. All of the Free Cinema shorts are featured on the *Free Cinema* DVD (BFI).

1956 First screening of Free Cinema short films at the *National Film Theatre* in London. All of the Free Cinema shorts are featured on the *Free Cinema* DVD (BFI).

1962 *La Jetée* (France) – Chris Marker's influential science fiction photomontage with a ice-over, telling the story of a bleak future after nuclear war. Only one shot moves and originates from a motion-picture camera.

1967 *The Big Shave* (USA) – Martin Scorsese's most famous short is an indictment of America's involvement in Vietnam, suggested by its alternative title *Viet '67*.
Electronic Labyrinth THX1138.4EB (USA) – George Lucas' thesis short film at the University of Southern California. He later developed it into a feature-length film – though many critics prefer the original short film.

1968 *Amblin'* (USA) – Stephen Spielberg first made his mark as a director with this 26-minute short film set in the desert.

1970 Home Box Office cable channel executive, Bernice Coe, creates slots for 'interstitial' shorts that 'make up the minutes' between the main attraction feature-length films so that movies can start on the hour, as is custom and practice with networked shows. This policy effectively creates a new market for short films in America.

1971 The UK's National Film School opens in London, co-funded by British film industry and the government. It becomes the National Film and Television School (NFTS) in 1982.

1981 Robert Redford founds the *Sundance Institute*, taking over the Utah Film Festival. The Sundance Film Festival is now considered to be the major festival for independent and short films in America.

1982 *An Exercise in Discipline – Peel* (AU) – Jane Campion's short film provides a close, concentrated look at a dysfunctional (or regular) family in a car. From the *Jane Campion: Three Short Films* (2000) DVD.

1989 *New York Stories* – Woody Allen, Francis Ford Coppola and Martin Scorsese pay tribute to New York City with three short films that are given a cinematic release in one programme.

1993 Tartan Shorts established, co-funded by Scottish Screen and BBC Scotland, with an annual showcase at the Edinburgh Festival and the *Cineworks* production funding initiative

1994 *The Wrong Trousers* (UK) – Nick Park of Aardman Animations in Bristol wins an Oscar for 'Best Short Film, Animated' and a BAFTA for 'Best Animated Film'.

1995 Foundation of the Brief Encounters International Film Festival in Bristol – the leading British showcase for short films.
Lumière and Company – a compilation of microshort films. Some of

the world's leading directors (David Lynch, Spike Lee, Wim Wenders, Zhang Yimou, etc) use the original Lumière picture camera to create short films. Each film is 52 seconds long, this being the amount of time it takes for one spool of film to run through their camera.

1997	*Gasman* (UK) – Lynne Ramsay, graduate of the UK's National Film and Television School, makes headlines with this award-winning short film.
1999	Atom Films' online portal is established. Short films are streamed to internet users through a pay-per-view subscription.
2001	UK Film Council establishes the New Cinema Fund to fund digitally shot films of less than 10 minutes in length and costing no more than £10,000. *Digital Shorts* (2004) is a compilation of selected highlights of the scheme, so is *Big Stories, Small Flashes* (2003).
2001	The world's first dedicated short film channel, *Moviola*, is launched in Canada.
2002	*11'09"01 – September 11* – this film comprises 11 short films, all 11 minutes and 9 seconds long and consisting of only 1 frame, by 11 directors from different countries and cultures.
2002	*In Short: A Guide to Short Film-making in the Digital Age* (Elsey and Kelly, BFI) – the first substantive exploration of the short film form.
2005	Short Film International Symposium at the Cork Film Festival. Festival director Mick Hannigan launches a 'search for 100 great films' at the Cannes Film Festival: *'This is not an attempt to establish a definitive canon of great shorts, but rather to champion and celebrate great examples of what we believe to be a critically neglected art form.'*
2006	First podcast short films become available on download to handheld devices such as PDAs and iPods.

Historical overview of the short film

● How to teach historical contexts

The following overview is intended as background information for the busy teacher seeking a selective history rather than as a model of knowledge and understanding to impart to students. However, a class research project into the history of the short film could usefully in contextualise some of the shorts used for textual analysis and provide a framework for the students' own practical production work.

Fact sheet: Short films by decade is a selected chronology of some key directors and films. Students might be asked to expand upon and complete this document through internet and other research. A decade-by-decade approach will offer a range of insights into the cinematic concerns and movements of particular times. Exploring the production contexts of particular short films will also provide information about the social and political histories of national cinemas.

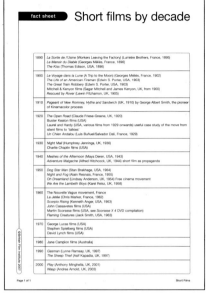

1 page

To access student worksheets and other online materials go to *Teaching Short Films* at **www.bfi.org.uk/tfms** and enter User name: **shorts@bfi.org.uk** and Password: **te1203sf**.

● **Early pioneers**

Short film has a history as old as film itself. The first films, from the earliest days of primitive cinema, were short (due to technological restrictions), experimental sequences that are very different from what we now consider films to be. These short films were silent, apart from the noise generated by the mechanical devices that enabled viewers to see them. Early short film was frequently no more than the (silent) recording of social events, such as *Sortie d'Usine (Workers Leaving the Factory*, France, 1895) by the brothers Louis and Auguste Lumière, showing approximately 100 workers at a factory for photographic goods in Lyon-Montplaisir leaving through two gates and exiting the frame to both sides.

From 1900 to 1913, filmmakers Sagar Mitchell and James Kenyon, commissioned by touring showmen, roamed the North of England, Scotland, Ireland and Wales to film the everyday lives of people at work and play. For around 70 years, 800 rolls of their early nitrate film sat in sealed barrels in the basement of a local shop in Blackburn. Miraculously discovered by a local businessman and painstakingly restored by the BFI, this ranks as the most exciting film discovery of recent times. The BFI has released two documentary-based DVD compilations of this work.

The role played by such early films merits closer attention, not least for their significant contribution to the development of the visual language and grammar of film that we have come to accept as conventional today. The BFI documentary *Silent Britain* released on DVD, offers an accessible overview of this period. BFI's Screenonline (www.screenonline.org.uk) features English films from this period, such as *Rescued by Rover*, in their entirety for free. The DVD compilation *Early Cinema: Primitives and Pioneers* (BFI) features a comprehensive selection of early films.

● Short film and Hollywood

Short film was soon eclipsed by the emergence of the dominant mode of film production: the classical narrative, feature-length film. This dominance was reinforced by the genre production of the Hollywood studio system and attempts by other national cinemas to compete with what has become the imperial currency of cinema admissions. Cinema exhibitors require films to conform to the 100-minute 'directive'. Under such circumstances, screenings can be scheduled in two-hour blocks, allowing customers time for visits to the concessions stands, and for viewing advertising and trailers for future releases. These factors mitigate against the visibility of short film within the mainstream of film exhibition. Thus, from the 1930s onwards, short film production, in commercial terms at least, became a marginalised activity, operating under budget constraints or only with the view to mainstream film production. Industrial factors influencing short film production led to the form occupying a near-invisible status within the realm of popular culture.

The Academy of Motion Picture Arts and Sciences (AMPAS) established awards (Oscars) for short films in 1932, but the categories in which they were to be judged – 'Short Subjects, comedy' and 'Short Subjects, novelty' – were indicative of the form's marginalisation within the industry. Nowadays Hollywood no longer follows the studio system of production, it tends to see short film as a cut-price laboratory for experimentation and innovation where risks can be taken without a negative impact on the financial return of feature films. Studios have now developed a system of scouting new directorial talent emerging from the independent film scene and the numerous festivals where new and innovative films are showcased.

● Experimental/*avant-garde*/arthouse short films

While the short film form failed to compete with feature-length films, it found alternative arenas in which to operate, often away from the mainstream. Where short film struggled to establish itself in terms of entertainment, it had all the qualities that were desirable for film to be regarded as art. It was readily accessible to artists with a moderate income, who could share ideas within creative co-operatives and societies. Avant-garde and experimental cinemas have traditionally taken a strong interest in short film, but opportunities for the theatrical exhibition of non-narrative film dwindled from the 1950s onwards and remain very limited within the mainstream. Maya Deren's experimental films, from the early 1940s until her death in 1961, display a highly individualistic sensibility towards the form of the short film. Her film Meshes of the Afternoon (USA, 1943) set the tone for American avant-garde filmmaking and remains an important influence on contemporary independent filmmakers. Deren is frequently cited as an example of a filmmaker who has taken an anti-mainstream stance in the 'artistic licence and creative freedom' versus 'commercial pressures' debate.

● Short film and protest/Free cinema

One notable form of protest to the dominance of the mainstream was that of the British Free Cinema movement of the 1950s. This topic would be a valuable case study of short film as counter cinema.

As John Ellis writes in his online article about the movement:

> It was an opposition to the monopoly operating in film distribution, and the refusal of producers and distributors to consider films which were different, controversial. Here was involved not only the radical demand for an 'independent cinema', using 16mm rather than35 mm (still considered an 'amateurs' gauge') but also a concern to show that good films were just as (if not more) likely to be made on small budgets as large. (www.bfi.org.uk/features/freecinema/archive/ellis-freecinema.html)

Most of the films from this influential movement are short films. They had in common not only the conditions of their production (shoestring budget, unpaid crew) and the equipment they employed (usually hand-held 16mm Bolex cameras), but also a style and attitude, and an experimental approach to sound. Mostly funded by the BFI's Experimental Film Fund and the Ford Motor Company, they featured ordinary, mostly working-class people at work and play, displaying a rare sympathy and respect, and a self-consciously poetic style. The Free Cinema DVD box set (BFI) is a very useful source of these short films, which influenced the later British social realist movement and its feature-length productions.

There has been little academic work in documenting the role of short film as an agent of social change. The recent phenomenon of video activism has a symbiotic relationship with short film and the production of 'witness videos' is a common strategy for protest groups, such as anti-hunting campaigners. Combining the traditions of cinéma vérité with direct political action, video activism produces footage that most usually finds its audience through news broadcast. However, organisations such as Amnesty International and Greenpeace frequently commission specialist-subject short films with a persuasive intent, and there are numerous film festivals showcasing 'political' short films.

● Short film on television

In the 1960s, television seemed to promise the potential for a more stable market for short film, but this proved to be a false dawn – the more homogenised and commercially viable products of the documentary and the drama series came to dominate the schedules throughout the 1970s and 1980s. There were a number of respected short film series, but these never had the exposure or effect attained by television plays, such as *Cathy Come Home* (Ken Loach, UK, 1966) for instance. Short films became minority viewing, scheduled into 'filler' and late-night slots, and their presence in the schedules was more likely attributable to the enterprise and zeal of individual directors, rather than the commissioning agency of the television industry.

The BBC2 series 10x10, developed in association with the BFI, was a staple of short film in the 1990s in Britain. This strand succeeded in providing a limited number of directors with the chance to produce and broadcast films of professional quality.

In 1993, the BBC launched its populist mass observation strand of short filmmaking, *Video Nation*, which focuses on close-up talking heads with straight to camera narration. As video cameras became smaller and easier to use during the 1980s and 1990s, video diaries became a popular format. *Video Nation*, started by Chris Mohr and Mandy Rose, distributed Hi-8 cameras across the UK for one year to get people to film their everyday lives. The BBC received thousands of entries, from which approximately 1300 shorts were edited and shown on television. The popularity of the format (viewing figures varied from 1 million to 9 million) led to some themed series of *Video Nation* shorts such as *African Shorts*, *Hong Kong Shorts*, *Coming Clean* (a 10-part series on housework), *Bitesize Britain* (ten 15-minute programmes about what the nation really eats) and many more. With a massive take-up rate, establishing the video diary form that was to influence the later generation of reality TV, the project went online in 2001 (www.bbc.co.uk/videonation).

Video Diaries is another BBC series centred around video diaries, though this series tends to feature eccentrics or people with social problems. People who are chosen to do a video diary are given rudimentary training, and a BBC producer guides them through the process of shooting and editing their contributions. In the context of mainstream television it is obviously wise to have such guidance, even though the programmes are 'sold' as being raw slices of life.

These initiatives were the exception rather than the rule, however, as television producers and cinemas distributors alike found the form to be problematic in terms of scheduling. Only at the start of the 20th century has this picture started to change, with the proliferation of channels through cable television. In Britain, Film 4 is now free-to-air. It operates a policy of repeating broadcasts for its *Core Shorts* and themed sequences of short films in its *Shooting Gallery* series. The BBC has established its Film Network as an online portal as well as a feeder organisation for its terrestrial programming. The world's first dedicated short film channel, *Moviola*, was launched in Canada in 2001 and there are plans for this to be made more widely available and eventually to establish a global service.

● Short film production and education

A factor to consider in this regard is the only recent availability of products on DVD and digital formats.

Specialist film and art-school courses in the higher education sector aside, (according to Edmond Levy's research, New York University makes 4,000 short films a year) the realm of media education has only fairly recently turned its attention to the short film form. Perhaps teachers are turning to the short film partially in response to increasingly pressured examination specifications. It is surprising that it has taken so long for the short film to be taken up as a medium for learning, given its particular advantages for practical work. Short film production is collaborative, creative, and learners may take an idea from script to screen acting as a microcosm of a film production company. Student productions offer a chance for participants to understand the complexities behind film production as a learning exercise in its own right. Furthermore, there is a greater likelihood of a successful outcome than some of the more over-reaching projects that schools have embarked upon. Most post-16 and degree level courses in film now offer opportunities for practical work, such as short filmmaking, and this is the most frequently cited reason for students choosing courses of this type.

In Britain, the National Film and Television School (NFTS) has established a reputation as the UK's national centre of excellence for education in film and TV programme-making. It has been running specialist courses in writing, directing and producing short films and television programmes since 1970 and its graduates frequently enter the field of professional filmmaking. A lot of the NFTS's short films are entered into festivals or find an audience through the school's partnerships with the BBC, Film 4, Aardman Animations, MTV and Kaos films.

Skillset is the Sector Skills Council for the Audio Visual Industries (broadcast, film, video, interactive media and photo imaging). Jointly funded by industry and government, their job is to make sure that the UK audio-visual industries have the right people, with the right skills, in the right place, at the right time, so that Britain's industries remain competitive. Skillset conducts consultation work with industry, publishes research and strategic documents, runs funding schemes and project work, and provides impartial media careers advice for aspiring new entrants and established industry professionals. Skillset is a useful organisation to contact for information on short film production and ways forward after a short film is completed. Further information about this organisation can be found in the resources section.

● Short film as 'calling card' for the industry

The contemporary film industry is geared towards its preferred form (the feature-length film) for production and distribution and the relationship with the short film scene is understood variously as paternalistic or exploitative, depending on the perspective of the commentator. Certainly, industrial imperatives and institutional determinants are key factors of which short filmmakers must be aware if they are to use their productions as a springboard into the film business.

There are now funding institutions such as Film 4 and the UK Film Council who see in short film a possibility to succinctly represent social issues and provide disenfranchised communities with a voice. Both public and private companies are keen to be seen to have addressed the social-inclusion agenda set by the government and short film is a cost-effective way of allowing up-and-coming British ethnic talent to have a voice. Asif Kapadia is a young East-Londoner of Asian descent who started his career with making short films through state-supported production schemes. The success of his 1997 short film *The Sheep Thief* (UK) (on the *Cinema 16 – British Short Film* DVD), made while a student at the Royal College of Art and distributed by The Bureau, led to Film 4 finance for the feature-length production *The Warrior* (UK, 2001). Asif Kapadia, Yousaf Ali Khan and Amit Kumar are all short filmmakers of the 1990s who have moved towards feature film production as their careers have progressed, and who make suitable case studies for students.

The digital age: A brighter future for short film?

● Production

Digital technologies not only change the modes of production, they also change the modes of film consumption and the ways in which audiences interact with texts. Short films in the digital age are able to gain the exposure that they have been denied as broadband technology becomes more widely adopted. The proliferation of special-interest channels on cable television has also seen a surge of interest in the short film form and greater opportunities for projects to be green-lighted as there is less capital at risk. Recently, there has been an enhanced interest in the untapped potential of the short film form and it has even been mooted that it might become the saviour of the British national cinema.

It was this belief that prompted the UK Film Council to launch their three-year scheme to support digital short films in August 2001, pledging £1.5 million to produce 100 films each year as part of its *Digital Shorts* initiative. Funds were to be matched by regional partners, each film was to be shot solely on digital for less than £10,000, and each had to be less than ten minutes long. Successful short films delivered by directors funded by this strategy, such as *Wasp* (Andrea Arnold, UK, 2003) are considered to be the launching-pad for a new stream of filmmaking talent. Many critics have commented on the influence of this production strategy on Arnold's feature-length debut *Red Road* (UK, 2006).

The digital revolution is having an explosive impact on the short film scene. Where filmmaking used to be a highly expensive enterprise, the comparatively easy affordability of the means of production from the 1990s onwards has empowered new generations of filmmakers. Much has been made of the potential of 'democratic cameras' and of films promoting particular social agendas. See *The Video Activist Handbook* (2001) by Thomas Harding for more information about this field. When the concern with social issues is combined with the speed of production of digital filmmaking, there is an increased likelihood of short film serving the interests of society.

Many first-world national cinemas, most notably Britain, Australia and America, see short film as part of their heritage but have given scant regard to the form over the years in comparison with star-driven and feature-length film. Government agencies have typically engaged with short filmmaking in two ways: as a talent-spotting mechanism and as a training ground for feature-length production. In Britain, the UK Film Council is the government-backed strategic agency for film, which

> ...aims to stimulate a successful, vibrant film industry and to promote the widest possible enjoyment and understanding of cinema throughout the UK.

It does this through supporting a number of production schemes:

- The New Cinema Fund Digital Shorts initiative: awarding grants of £10,000 for digital short films through a number of regional agencies.
- First Light: this scheme's objective is to create opportunities for children and young people of school age to make short films and is able to make an impact upon social inclusion and cultural and ethnic diversity objectives. For more details go to: www.firstlightmovies.com.

- Cinema Extreme: in collaboration with Film 4 and The Bureau, this scheme aims to encourage and develop filmmakers with a distinctive directorial voice and cinematic flair.

The UK Film Council has also funded the production and retail distribution of two compilation DVDs that showcase the most successful short films from these schemes:

- *Big Stories, Small Flashes* (2003)
- *Digital Shorts* (2004).

These short films are frequently toured as a programme to regional cinemas as *Digital Shorts.* The UK Film Council's schemes have been criticised for prioritising the funding of politically correct and worthy films on topics such as immigration, which push the government's agenda rather than genuinely making a difference to the beleaguered UK film industry. Most of these accusations point to the poor return of taxpayers' money and of lottery funding, in developing new directors who make the step up to feature-length film. Rarely do the critics of the schemes recognise the longer-term benefits of supported production of short films or the strengths of individual productions in their own terms.

● Online distribution

As broadband technology extended to the home-market in the early 2000s, a new generation of web surfers were able to access short films and to upload their productions to find an audience. Atom Films quickly established itself as the market leader in the provision of an online portal service, building a platform for artists seeking worldwide distribution. The BBC has established the Film Network for short film (there are case studies of these two institutions in Section 3), and there are numerous other examples of online short film portals, some more quality-oriented than others.

● Marketing short film products to niche markets

Future Shorts is marketing short film compilations in much the same way that record companies released records in the 1970s and 1980s, producing limited editions whose exclusivity made them desirable. (See page 64.)

Chris Morris' *My Wrongs* (UK, 2002) is a rare example of a short film that was commercially successful, selling 12,000 copies when it was released on DVD in 2004. As a first foray into film production by dance-record label Warp, it paved the way for Chris Cunningham's *Rubber Johnny* (UK, 2005) and Paul Fraser's short *Scummy Man* (UK, 2006) (which had a budget of £60,000) – based on the Arctic Monkeys' song 'When the Sun Goes Down'. To explore the limited number of single short film releases with your class, see **Worksheet 15**.

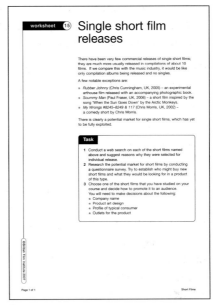

worksheet 15 **Single short film releases**

There have been very few commercial releases of single short films; they are much more usually released in compilations of about 10 films. If we compare this with the music industry, it would be like only compilation albums being released and no singles.

A few notable exceptions are:

▪ *Rubber Johnny* (Chris Cunningham, UK, 2005) – an experimental arthouse film released with an accompanying photographic book.
▪ *Scummy Man* (Paul Fraser, UK, 2006) – a short film inspired by the song 'When the Sun Goes Down' by the Arctic Monkeys.
▪ *My Wrongs #8245–8249 & 117* (Chris Morris, UK, 2002) – a comedy short by Chris Morris.

There is clearly a potential market for single short films, which has yet to be fully exploited.

Task

1 Conduct a web search on each of the short films named above and suggest reasons why they were selected for individual release.
2 Research the potential market for short films by conducting a questionnaire survey. Try to establish who might buy new short films and what they would be looking for in a product of this type.
3 Choose one of the short films that you have studied on your course and decide how to promote it to an audience. You will need to make decisions about the following:
  ▪ Company name
  ▪ Product art design
  ▪ Profile of typical consumer
  ▪ Outlets for the product

©British Film Institute 2007

Page 1 of 1   Short Films

1 page

To access student worksheets and other online materials go to *Teaching Short Films* at **www.bfi.org.uk/tfms** and enter User name: **shorts@bfi.org.uk** and Password: **te1203sf**.

The *Best v Best* DVD compilation (UK, 2005), produced by Shooting People, had an initial run of only 2000 copies. *Best v Best* features seven award-winning shorts, including the BAFTA-winning *The Banker* (Hattie Dalton, UK, 2005), Oscar-nominated *Little Terrorist* (Ashvin Kumar, India/UK, 2004), and Sundance-winning short documentary *Family Portrait* (Rob Brown, UK, 2005). Although it is aiming for a broad audience, *Best v Best* is not available in high-street shops. As its distributor says

> You just get buried. The deals are rotten, it's a huge amount of work, and you don't get much return. We get a much, much better return by selling it ourselves online or through specialist stores such as that at the Institute of Contemporary Art.

● The film festival circuit and cinematic exhibition

Film festival screenings are by far the most likely way that short filmmakers can secure the cinematic exhibition of their films; yet here, also, it is institutional determinants that pose major constraints. The festival circuit, increasingly providing exhibition possibilities for no-budget and low budget short films, is a burgeoning service industry that taps into a stream of creativity often ignored by the majors. UK-based festivals such as Brief Encounters, First Light, Exposures, Bang! And Raindance are all recent initiatives that provide a forum for bringing audiences, short filmmakers and industry representatives together. There are many more such initiatives worldwide. To explore short film festivals with your class, see **Worksheets 18 and 19**.

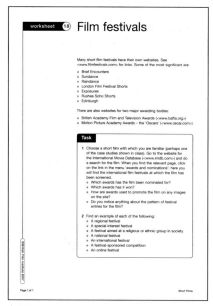

1 page

1 page

Cinematic exhibition beyond the festival circuit is highly unlikely for the vast majority of short films, and the biggest challenge for the short filmmaker still is to secure theatrical distribution. The most visible outlet for a short film is to be programmed alongside a feature, but this is an increasingly rare phenomenon, particularly in the days of multiplex domination. *Desserts* (Jeff Stark, UK, 1998), for example, saw a national release alongside the feature film *Divorcing Jack* (David Caffrey, UK, 1998). *Desserts* can now be viewed on the web outlet Beam TV: www.beam.tv/beamreels/reel_player.php?reel=wwRjKmmnPQ&reel_file=vVCkZJxPwm&fs=1.

● Convergence of media forms

Short film has proved itself to be the perfect form of entertainment for the mobile devices that are now so popular. A growing number of start-up companies are involved in the production, distribution and exhibition of short films. To explore some of these companies with your class, research the ones listed on **Worksheet 16**. It is interesting to note how many communications companies have been involved in the sponsorship of digital short film competitions and festivals. Orange, for example, has sponsored the Depict! 90-second film competition and Nokia has developed its own shorts competition through its website. These companies are aware of the viral marketing strategies that take advantage of counter-cultural spoofs of mainstream advertising. They seek to profit from the cost of sending short film files from one user to another.

To access student worksheets and other online materials go to *Teaching Short Films* at **www.bfi.org.uk/tfms** and enter User name: **shorts@bfi.org.uk** and Password: **te1203sf**.

1 page

● **Podcasting**

The development of MP3 players has transformed the ways in which music is purchased and consumed – digital files of songs are imported to the handset through a connection to the internet. The release of the Apple iPod has gone on to revolutionise several industries and makes a fascinating case study of how new technology can have a powerful effect on society. The introduction of the fifth generation iPod, with its video capability and colour screen, perhaps sees the iPod set to revolutionise the short film industry in the way it has the music industry. Two important factors will have an impact on the consumption of short film, time-shifting and place-shifting, and both are linked to the portability of the product. The decision to make the software Synch Home Movies available as a free download from iTunes is a strategic one on the part of Apple. This package will allow digital short filmmakers to upload their productions to the iTunes site and find 'free' audiences. In the first instance, the films are being offered at no cost, in order to build a user-base, but it is probable that they will be sold in the future.

Certainly, the hardware on which short film production relies is becoming increasingly accessible in the twenty-first century, as is its ease of use. Furthermore, technological developments points towards a device that unifies and integrates the means of production, distribution and exhibition. The integrated, hand held device that functions as a portable means of communication, information, entertainment (audio and visual) source, camera recorder and telephone, is not far from being developed and marketed, and we can expect a further revolution in how short film will be perceived within such an age. Short film will have an exciting future as we move towards that date.

3

Case studies

The following case study focus in depth on a selected short film and are supported by a range of handouts and additional materials. For each of the short films suggested in Scheme of work 1, viewing notes providing further contextual information are available for students. To provide students with contextual information on each of the case study films, see **Viewing notes 1–4**. These can be accessed as part of the online materials at www.bfi.org.uk/tfms.

At the centre of any study of short film is likely to be the textual analysis of professionally produced texts that illustrate its basic conventions. As there are many forms of short film and little space here, I have concentrated on live-action drama.

Case study 1: Short film and film language

This case study focuses in depth on *About a Girl* (Brian Percival, UK, 2001) and is designed to supply teachers with a clear model for teaching film language through close textual analysis (known as micro analysis in the WJEC Film Studies specification) broadly covering the following areas:

- Cinematography
- *Mise en scène*
- Editing
- Sound (dialogue, sound effects and music).

Introduce your students to textual analysis of a short film by modelling the deconstruction of a chosen text. Students should be made aware that filmmaking involves a sequence of choices and decisions, and that even very short films are complex texts rich in generating meanings for viewers. For this reason, micro shorts are a particularly useful starting point. A screening of any of the Nokia 15-second finalists' films on the *Best of 13th Raindance Film Festival Shorts* DVD or from the Depict! website (also available on their compilation DVD) such as *Le Cheval 2.1* (Stephen S Haywood and Kirk

Kirkland, UK, 2005) from the 2003 shortlist, *Non-Fat* (Oliver Manzi, UK, 2004) from the 2004 shortlist, and other micro shorts such as *Desserts*, will give students a sense of how short films can quickly capture the attention of an audience.

The first time that a film is screened, it is recommended that the teacher does little to contextualise or introduce the film – viewers should not pre judge films, but be allowed to form their own opinions. It is helpful to move from a straightforward denotation exercise (getting students to describe what they see in still images, using the remote control to freeze frame moments) to connotation work (getting students to suggest meanings that the text might produce), as this encourages individual learner's appreciation of film. It might be useful to employ class brainstorm activities, where individuals make points that are put up on the board, grouped under headings. Make students aware that they will have a chance to analyse short films of their own choosing and that this activity equips them with the skills and specialist vocabulary to be able to do this to a high standard.

It is important at this point to remind students that micro shorts serve different intentions and audiences than their more usual diet of feature-length, Hollywood products. A short discussion on micro shorts and emerging technologies, such as webcasting and podcasting, allows students an opportunity to adjust their expectations about this form of film. **Worksheet 1** can then be used as a follow-up activity within the lesson or as homework. Alternatively, some of the tasks can be prepared as board work and class activities where students can contribute their ideas in a forum of their peers.

Worksheet 2 provides a framework for analysing a film as a whole and encourages learners to consider how particular moments in a film are key to how the film is read. This worksheet covers key concepts and features of films that will provide learners with ways in to the film and provide points for sharing with peers in class. The worksheet also encourages learners to record key information about the film (title, director, country and year of production and synopsis). These worksheets might be used for each film viewed and be included in a viewing log, a useful *aide mémoire*.

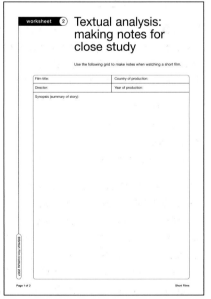

1 of 2 pages

1 of 2 pages

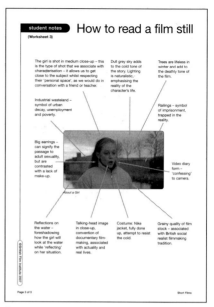

1 page

To access student worksheets and other online materials go to *Teaching Short Films* at **www.bfi.org.uk/tfms** and enter User name: **shorts@bfi.org.uk** and Password: **te1203sf**.

In the next lesson, students should work in pairs to analyse selected images from **Worksheet 3.** These activities work towards revealing the range of choices available to the filmmaker in the construction or composition of images. In selecting three images from the ten provided, students should be advised to select stills that serve different functions within the film. **Worksheet 3** includes the handout **How to read a film still**, which provides a model for the close analysis of the images. The activities are framed around the focus text *About a Girl* and move learners from denotation (describing) activities to connotation (suggesting meanings) work, so that the notion of individual interpretation of images can be foregrounded. In order to encourage your students to further consider how images work in relation to each other within films, and to offer a practical explication of the theory covered in the image-analysis task, **Worksheet 4** provides a photo shoot task, framed from the perspective of a male character.

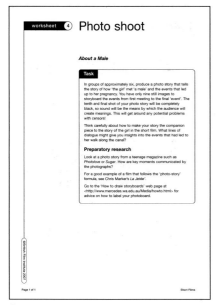

1 page

About a Girl

This short film can be found on the BFI's *Moving Shorts* DVD and on the *Cinema 16 – British Short Films* DVD, with a director and scriptwriter commentary option.

Julie Rutterford wrote the screenplay after being disturbed by an article in *The Guardian* about Britain's high rates of teenage pregnancy and the apparent lack of interest in the human stories behind the government statistics. Rutterford had previously forged a career in television soap operas such as *Brookside* and the drama series *Teachers*, so was well positioned to develop the dramatic potential of the story. The idea took several years to gestate while Rutterford repositioned the script and drew on media debates about single parents and teenage pregnancy and to tie in references to popular culture. In presenting one of the numerous awards the film won, producer Stephen Woolley pointed to its '*witty, charming script and truly shocking punchline*' as key factors in the judges' decision.

The opening-title sequence of the film sees the words *About a Girl* displayed for the audience letter by letter in the text font associated with mobile phones. The audio track uses the sound of a dial-up connection. Thus, the film is immediately associated with emerging technologies and youth culture. The film employs a common stereotype of contemporary teenagers who 'never stop using their phones'; we see the girl looking at her mobile phone later in the film and can speculate on whom she is communicating with. Furthermore, the film's title is an example of intertextuality in that it creates a point of contrast with a more mainstream product, that of the popular Nick Hornby novel *About a Boy* (2000), later made into a film *About a Boy* (Chris and Paul Weitz, UK, 2002) as a star vehicle for Hugh Grant.

In terms of production values and the representation of social issues, the two films are at opposite ends of the filmmaking spectrum. *About a Girl* was debuting in short film festivals around the world at the same time as the feature film was being marketed and might have attracted some audiences through its ability to present an alternative viewpoint to the upbeat closure of *About a Boy*.

Told from the point of view of a 13-year-old girl, this short film shows her hopes and dreams to be in direct opposition to the realities of her northern, working-class life. As she sings Britney Spears' lyrics 'I'm not that innocent' from her hit song 'Oops! ... I Did It Again', the words underline unhappy ironies in relation to the events of her own life. To explore the use of sound and music in *About a Girl*, see **Worksheet 6**. As the girl relays scenes from her ordinary teenage life, there is an uncomfortable sense of sadness underlying her easy-going tales, but it is not until the end that we find out the disturbing truth.

The film commences with an establishing long shot that sees the girl on a grassy hillside silhouetted against a cloudy summer sky. We see her practising her dance moves; the routine taken from the Britney Spears' video for her song *Stronger*. The shot is taken from a low angle and the girl is framed against a passionate sky of summer storm clouds. The dark silhouette might be read as symbolic of the dark secrets of her teenage life. To further explore the cinematography of particular scenes from the film in this manner, see **Worksheet 5**.

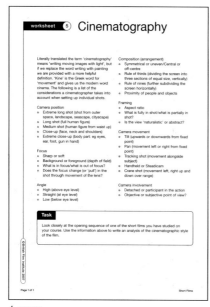

1 page

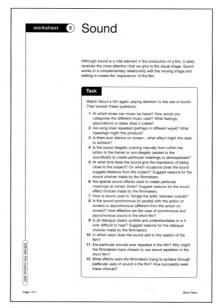

1 page

The opening line of the film's central monologue (which gives the film its structure) immediately hooks the audience into the character of the girl. 'If Jesus were alive today, right, he'd probably be a singer. He'd be like Bono, only with hair.' Her colloquial delivery masks a clever amalgamation of several of the film's themes: death, sin and suffering and teenage popular culture, but its fast-paced delivery allows us no time for reflection on these issues. The line is delivered directly to camera, in the style of recent youth television programmes. However, the film draws on several other familiar forms of genre storytelling to achieve its effect. To more fully explore the notion of film genres with your class, see **Worksheet 11**, though it might be more appropriate to address this topic within the second scheme of work.

To access student worksheets and other online materials go to *Teaching Short Films* at **www.bfi.org.uk/tfms** and enter User name: **shorts@bfi.org.uk** and Password: **te1203sf**.

1 page

About a Girl cleverly plays with notions of genre and might be characterised in relation to the following forms:

Teen drama *About a Girl* might be considered to set itself in opposition to popular American teen drama series such as *Dawson's Creek* and their British counterparts like *Hollyoaks*. It does, however, share points of similarity, in focusing on the lives of young people who are set apart from the adult worlds of their parents and in dealing with the problematic passage to adulthood.

Video diary The video diary emerged from the availability of cheaper camcorders in the 1980s and became a popular and low-cost way of capturing the aesthetics of first-person work. Successful projects were broadcast on BBC platforms through series such *Video Nation* and the *Capture Wales* digital storytelling project. The confessional tone of this form of loose documentary has been further formalised in the reality TV programmes of the 1990s, such as the *Big Brother* diary room/confessional booth.

Documentary Short films that seek to comment on social deprivation have a long history that can be traced back such seminal films like *Housing Problems*

(Edgar Anstley, Arthur Elton, UK, 1935) (available on the BFI *Real Shorts* DVD). Director Brian Percival spent time in scoping out locations that would bring a sense of actuality to *About a Girl*. He states in the director's commentary on the DVD that he

> … wanted to get the feeling that we were almost shooting documentary. Although it was all scripted – all the monologue lines were written out, there were a few improvisations to make it feel real, to try to make the feel almost documentary level.

Comedy *About a Girl* has some similarities with *The Fast Show* (BBC, 1994–2000): the 'Brilliant!' spoof-youth-presenting of Paul Whitehouse, and Caroline Aherne's teenage-girl monologues. There are also similarities between the character of 'the girl' and the Vicky Pollard character from *Little Britain* (BBC, 2003–present). The character of Vicky Pollard has captured the imagination of young people as an example of a 'chav'. The use of this word, an abbreviation of 'council house and violent' has entered the vocabulary of the media and is now used frequently as a term of abuse by (and to) young people. The short film *How to be the Perfect Chav* made by Lucy Whiteside and Kellie Munckton, two 17 year olds, in Somerset, is available at: www.youtube.com/watch?v=ZdNfFwi3YLU.

A comic effect is achieved at times in *About a Girl*, for example when the girl uses 'Not!' after her statement about her father's claim: 'He could've played for City. Not!' This is indicative of the common language of 'youthspeak', with this particular use of language entering popular discourse after the release of the American teen comedy *Wayne's World* (Penelope Spheeris, USA, 1992).

Teachers can print out the complete dialogue of the short film from the transcript on the BFI *Moving Shorts* website (only accessible with a password, which is supplied with the *Moving Shorts* DVD).

British social realism

If British cinema can be considered to have a strong identity then it is commonly associated with the social realist film tradition. *About a Girl* is indebted to the films of earlier directors such as Lindsay Anderson and Karel Reisz, and more recent releases by the likes of Ken Loach and Mike Leigh. Films of this nature tend to focus on themes of social injustice, adopt a critical stance in regard to contemporary politics and use filmstock that creates the grainy images audiences associate with actuality filmmaking. The film was shot around the Miles Platting and Newton Heath areas in north Manchester, whose communities that have many problems with poverty, crime and drugs.

The producer, Janey de Nordwall, decided to work with unknown actors as part of the attempt to underline the realism of the story. The film stars 13-year-old newcomer Ashley Thewlis in a performance that Ewan McGregor described as 'very hard hitting and brilliant, brilliant, brilliant' in his tribute at the Turner Classic Movies awards at the London Film Festival in 2002. Despite her recognisable surname, being a distant relation of the successful British actor David Thewlis, she had yet to appear in any acting role on screen. Ashley had been picked up by a casting agency and scheduled to appear in the TV series *Cops* to play a teenage prostitute, but this hadn't been released. In order to elicit the performance from Ashley they rehearsed so much that the girl could actually walk down the street in Manchester and she would be in character.

> We found Ashley, the girl, when she was unknown and it was only her second time in front of a camera. However, she was a natural, she had instant character and her presence was magnetic. We spent a lot of time improvising in rehearsals with the other actors to help build her character, and to help her to understand her motivation. I had to be able to believe in this character, I had to be able to believe that Ashley was the girl walking alongside the canal and I had to trick the audience into thinking they knew her too. That was the challenge. (Brian Percival in the director's commentary).

● Popular culture

The monologue of 'the girl' makes numerous references to figures from contemporary popular culture: Bono, Madonna, Kelly from Stereophonics, Kurt Cobain – 'him in Nirvana'. Young people remain the most important consumers of popular music and frequently define themselves in relation to the types of songs to which they listen. The pleasures young people derive from popular culture and pop stars through fan discourses are referred to throughout the film. The monologue includes use of the abbreviations for the names of her friends Kelly P and Kelly T who, along with Meera, will form the four-piece girl group imagined by the central protagonist. This is an allusion to the Spice Girls and the notion of female empowerment (or Girl Power). It would be easy to dismiss the girl's seemingly immature reference to gender representation and sexual politics, but such issues have to be seen in the real social contexts of teenage girls.

The lyrics from Britney Spears' songs 'Oops! … I Did It Again' and 'Stronger' (a full transcript of the lyrics of each of these songs is available in **Viewing notes 1**), from her 2000 album *Oops! … I Did It Again*, take on a new dimension in the context of the film. Britney was particularly popular with the target audience of teenage girls who have followed her own transition from teen star to adult entertainer. The release of 'I'm Not a Girl, Not Yet a Woman' in 2001 sees further parallels between the girl and the evolving identity of her idol. At the time of the film's production, Britney was famous for still being a virgin, giving these songs an ironic dimension, which might be less obvious today, when motherhood rather than virginity is more a part of Britney's image.

To access student worksheets and other
online materials go to *Teaching Short Films*
at **www.bfi.org.uk/tfms** and enter
User name: **shorts@bfi.org.uk** and
Password: **te1203sf**.

1 of 6 pages

● Director

Director Brian Percival began his working life as a city planner in Liverpool in
the early 1980s. He comments in an interview:

> I was given the consummate responsibility of deciding where to plant
> trees in a post riot torn Toxteth. This involved drawing little squiggly
> circles on a large-scale street map. It was Michael Heseltine's solution to
> restoring racial and class harmony in the Inner Cities ... (from
> www.bigfishmanagement.com/brianpercival/)

Deciding there was probably little future in this, Percival moved to London and
enroled at art school. It was there that he developed a passion for photography
and later for 8mm film. After graduating from film school he trod the well-worn
path through music/fashion clips and onto TV commercials. For the first time
in his life he was being paid to do something he loved. He started investigating

> what it was that made some pictures good and others bad? Why is it
> that some pictures demand an emotional response? Something you just
> can't help but react to? It's still with me today, and never fails to
> confound how many elements can be built into an image to achieve the
> required response, albeit in ads, movies or magazines. (Ibid)

Percival learned his craft making TV commercials, music and fashion clips.
About a Girl was his first short film. Other directing credits include a series of
Clocking Off (BBC, 2000–5), *North and South* (BBC, 2004–present) and the
BBC version of *Much Ado about Nothing* (2005) with Billie Piper. Brian Percival

chose to shoot such a gritty script for his first short film as a backlash against the glossy commercialism of the adverts he had worked on before:

> It was as far removed from my advertising work as it can get, or maybe even a kick off against it. For some reason the idea of a purely character led performance really allowed me to again find something new in my approach to work. That's something I hope will always stay with me. (Ibid)

● Cinematography

The cinematographer (or Director of Photography or DP) for this film was Geoff Boyle who previously worked extensively in television commercials and music video. **Worksheet 5** addresses the choices available to a cinematographer. He used this film as a stepping stone to feature-length work and went on to work for Jean Jacques Arnaud in *Enemy at the Gates* (DL/GB/IE/USA/FR, 2001) (see Boyle's CV and read an interview with him at www.cinematography.net). Boyle comments on the difference from working on commercial projects:

> It was a real struggle, not lighting everything beautifully. Every shot was lit, but Brian and I found ourselves constantly reminding each other 'It's not a commercial' as an idea for a shot would appear and then be rejected. (from www.bigfishmanagement.com/brianpercival/).

About a Girl was shot on Super 16 over one week at the canalside in Manchester. Boyle explains the process of shooting on filmstock and then working on the film digitally in post production:

> My life was made hugely easier by the assistance of Digital Film Lab in London. We shot Super 16 and scanned on a Datacine at 2K conformed in Inferno and output to a 35mm neg. This enabled me to cope with the constantly changing light, we were shooting in winter in Manchester and the sun came out just as I needed overcast! We shaded the foreground on location and reduced contrast and saturation of the background in Datacine. (Ibid)

The film colour and light are used to evoke an emotional response, though this is done quite subtly as Boyle points out:

> The mood was meant to get darker as the story progressed but without telegraphing anything to the audience, just to influence them. We started heavily over filtering and then gradually reduced the filter combination so that we were almost uncorrected at the end. We then corrected these back to 'normal' which meant that we start with very little blue and end up with very little red. (Ibid)

● **Editing**

The pace of the editing in *About a Girl* is rapid and reflects the forms and conventions of broadcasting aimed at youth audiences, such as videos on MTV. To more fully explore the editing choices in the short film, see **Worksheet 7**. Percival states that they

> chose to cut [the film] primarily as a reflection of the quick way teenagers live their lives, 100 miles an hour, almost arbitrary thoughts.

worksheet ⑦ Editing

Transitions between shots of film are known as 'cuts' because in the early days of filmmaking, the film was literally cut and attached to the next piece of film. The creative use of transitions between shots is one of the key ways in which filmmakers create meanings. In the classic Hollywood style of filmmaking, transitions are intended to be smooth and seamless and do not draw attention to themselves. For this reason, the Hollywood style was said to use 'invisible editing'. Nowadays, there are many more types of transition than 'straight cuts' in a film (such as wipes, fades, dissolves, etc) and these have entered the 'grammar' of filmmaking over the years.

About a Girl is comprised of just over 100 visual edits, from its opening image to the last shot of the closing credits sequence.

Task

Watch the film once again, paying attention to the transitions between shots. Since the editing is so quick in places, you will need to pause the film as you work through it.

Now answer these questions:

1 Do all shots change with simple, straight cuts? When does the pattern of straight cuts change? Suggest reasons for the choices made by the film editor.
2 What is the pace of the editing like throughout the film? Does it speed up and slow down for particular scenes? Why might this be the case?
3 Are shots edited rapidly together to create a montage effect? Why do you think the filmmakers have employed this technique?
4 Does the editing remind you of any other film or television programme?
5 What types of transition other than straight cuts can you spot?
6 Do scenes fade out or run straight in to each other? What effect does this serve in the film as a whole?
7 Does the film use the cross-cutting technique (where the film cuts in turn between different times and places)? What effect is achieved through this?
8 Can the film be divided up into different types of sequence? How does the editing reflect these types of sequence?
9 How is sound used to 'bridge' the visual edits?

Page 1 of 1   Short Films

1 page

To access student worksheets and other online materials go to *Teaching Short Films* at **www.bfi.org.uk/tfms** and enter User name: **shorts@bfi.org.uk** and Password: **te1203sf**.

The film comprises 102 shots in its 9 minutes, 50 seconds, with 19 of these being flashbacks and 83 set in the contemporary moments of the walk along the canal path. The earlier tracking shots along the canal are edited to contrast with the reflective tone of the slower set pieces of the girl alone or with relatives. A sense of real time is provided by the continuous monologue of the voiceover, though this contrasts with the disruption of continuity afforded by the sudden shifts in location along the canalside and the flashback sequences that illustrate formative past events in the life of the girl. The final, climactic sequence is presented without comment, however, and this silence is only broken by her final line '*I'm still gonna have a 99*'; indicating a desire for comfort food and a reversion to the lost innocence of her childhood.

● Representation

The social group most clearly represented in *About a Girl* is that of the northern English working class and the film might be criticised for perpetuating stereotypes of urban communities: the settings, characters and their use of language, delivered fast-paced and with a thick Manchester accent, can be seen to portray the stereotypical working-class (or 'white trash' in popular parlance).

The father's character is revealed through his words and his actions. His reading the paper throughout the limited time he gets with his daughter and blowing mucus from his nose on the football pitch portray him as brutish and insensitive. (It has been suggested that the film alludes to child abuse by some viewers who have read into his portrayal the idea that he might be the father of the girl's baby.)

The film alludes, though indirectly, to the 'alcopops' debate, representing the girls' view on them as leading to a step up in society. Bacardi Breezer drinks are seen by the girl as the height of sophistication, something to aspire to, especially in comparison with the 'knock-off' lager her mum drinks. The girl wants out of her poor environment, refers to her mother as stingy and quotes her father calling her 'tight bitch'. Though we don't see how she lives, it is made clear where she comes from. In one of the flashback shots the girl is foregrounded looking at her mobile phone while her mother is seen scratching at a Lotto ticket. These scratch cards have been dubbed an 'idiot tax' on the poor or 'the only way out' for those trapped beneath the poverty line, and their inclusion in the film enhances its realistic representation of a contemporary working class family.

● Final sequence

The filmmakers deliberately bleached out the colours for the final sequence, giving it a much colder, harsher look. The final shot sees the girl walking away along the canal bank as the camera cranes upwards. A still image from this shot is available in the additional materials section (only accessible with a password) of the BFI *Moving Stories* website. She walks on the shadowy side of the canal, cut off from the sunnier side by the dark, foreboding water into which she has just thrown her carrier bag. The audience is left to consider the reasons for this shot. The camera drawing away indicates the closure of the narrative, but also heightens a sense of her smallness and insignificance against the landscape of urban deprivation – perhaps this can be read as a political comment. The crane shot might be read as forcing the audience into a judgment – we are no longer looking up at the girl, as in the opening image, but down at her – literally as well as metaphorically. Are we being drawn into making a judgment about her actions?

Worksheet 8 provides students with a structured group presentation activity, bringing together the topics encountered in Scheme of work 1. This will help students to develop the knowledge, understanding and skills with which to prepare individual textual analysis assignments. For a useful handout that provides a template for an extended essay, use **Worksheet 9**.

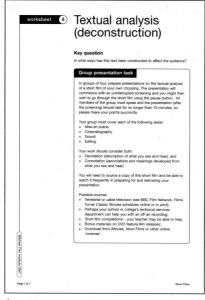

1 page

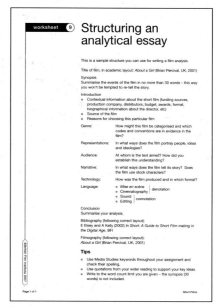

1 page

To access student worksheets and other online materials go to *Teaching Short Films* at **www.bfi.org.uk/tfms** and enter User name: **shorts@bfi.org.uk** and Password: **te1203sf**.

Case study 2: Short film and key concepts

This case study focuses in depth on *Two Cars, One Night* (Taika Waititi, 2003, New Zealand) and is supported by a range of handouts and additional materials. **Viewing notes 4** (at www.bfi.org.uk/tfms) provides further contextual information. The case study is designed to supply teachers with a clear model for teaching key concepts in moving image media through close textual analysis (known as micro analysis in the WJEC Film Studies specification), broadly framed around the following areas:

- Narrative and characterisation
- Genre – codes and conventions
- Representation
- Audiences.

● *Two Cars, One Night*

This short film can be found on the BFI *Moving Shorts* DVD and on the *Best v Best* DVD Vol One.

While waiting for their parents, two boys and a girl meet in the car park of a rural pub. What at first seems to be a relationship based on rivalry soon develops into a close friendship. We learn that love can be found in the most unlikely of places. The screenplay for this short film was written by Taika Waititi (aka Taika Cohen) who drew on his personal experiences as a child to create this story:

> There are a few moments in childhood that have a lasting impact. Not because they change the course of your life, or because they arrive with any great fanfare, in fact quite the opposite. Those are moments where an unexpected joy is found in the everyday, a moment of beauty in the ordinary. *Two Cars, One Night* captures one of those brief moments. The story, or rather the situation, has some personal significance for me as I spent many nights as a child in the confines of a large Holden car outside various pubs, waiting for adults to finish their business. For children, the dark world of grown-ups is a mysterious one. It is also very boring. You make your own fun, you invent games, you pick on each other, you pass the time, which can often be hours. (Taika Waititi from the film's website: www.twocarsonenight.com/).

The opening sequence of the film shows clouds moving across an evening sky, captured in black and white. The skyscape has been speeded up for the viewer and is accompanied by enigmatic music. The technique of speeding up cloud movement was famously used by Francis Ford Coppola in his teenage-gang film *Rumble Fish* (USA, 1983), shot in black and white, to signify the fast-paced life of the young protagonists. Coppola used it again in his more mainstream film *Jack* (USA, 1996), this time to signal the natural passage of time for Robin Williams' character who has an ageing disorder that sees him grow old four times faster than his peers. The skyscape shot in *Two Cars, One Night* also serves to locate the film in the country and culture of its origin for an international audience, as 'the land of the long white cloud' (*Aotearoa*) is the name given to New Zealand by the Maori.

The camera then tilts down from the night sky through a masked edit and seemingly the clouds, to an establishing shot of a car outside a remote motel. The soundtrack bridges these shots into the next; a mid-shot of the windscreen of the car, taken looking in at two young boys who are killing time waiting for their parents.

Next, several shots use special effects and time-lapse cinematography to illustrate the passage of time from the boys' point of view. The first picks up on the fast-forward of the introductory shot of the skyscape. Despite being speeded up, the viewer is able to imagine the length of time that has been represented in the shot, which sees several cars come and go, dropping off customers for the pub: many minutes in several seconds. The images are complemented with sound effects that include human speech on an audio track that has been speeded up – representing also how adult conversation can be just white noise to children.

A tracking shot runs along the side of the boys' car, taking its momentum from another car that is pulling in to stop at the next parking space – allowing the viewer to see two out-of-focus adults leaving the car to enter the pub. The shot creates a sense of involvement for the audience – we are positioned as if we are also in a vehicle, seeing the scene from that perspective. We notice a girl move from the backseat to the driver's position behind the wheel.

Next, a sequence of shot/reverse shot images initiates contact between the respective occupants of the two cars. Romeo, the elder boy of the two – shot from the girl's point of view – is jerked forward into side profile by the camera, while he is playing with the seat adjustor, pretending not to care about the girl. The action here provides the viewer with insights into character – Romeo's playfulness and acting 'cool' continues throughout the film, and so does that of the girl.

A later shot sees the girl yawning as a car passes in the background. The soundtrack has been edited very carefully here to synchronise the noise of the yawn and the sound of the car.

One of the advantages of short films is that they are not necessarily bound by the constraints of genre storytelling. *Two Cars, One Night* might have set itself up as a romance or love story in its tagline 'Love is found in the most unlikely of places' and its press pack synopsis 'A tale of first love', but it is the variation on the 'boy meets girl' story, relocating it to childhood, that gives the film its universality. To more fully explore narratives and plotlines with your class, see **Worksheet 10**. While the film positions itself as a romance in its tagline, audiences might have differing views on its genre. **Worksheet 11** considers aspects of genre in relation to the film and complicates the notion that the film is solely a romance.

Two Cars, One Night can be read as a statement about the generation gap, but director Taika Waititi claims on the film's website to be more interested in making comments about the universality of the human condition than criticising absentee parents:

> I do not seek to vilify adults or make presumptions about rural life. I want to show how human contact creates something special in a not so special environment.

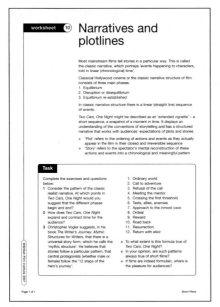

worksheet **10** **Narratives and plotlines**

Most mainstream films tell stories in a particular way. This is called the classic narrative, which portrays 'events happening to characters, told in linear (chronological) time'.

Classical Hollywood cinema or the classic narrative structure of film consists of three main phases:
1. Equilibrium
2. Disruption or disequilibrium
3. Equilibrium re-established

In classic narrative structure there is a linear (straight line) sequence of events.

Two Cars, One Night might be described as an 'extended vignette' – a short sequence, a snapshot of a moment in time. It displays an understanding of the conventions of storytelling and has a structured narrative that works with audiences' expectations of plots and stories.

• 'Plot' refers to the ordering of actions and events as they actually appear in the film in their closed and irreversible sequence
• 'Story' refers to the spectator's mental reconstruction of these actions and events into a chronological and meaningful pattern

Task

Complete the exercises and questions below:
1 Consider the pattern of the classic realist narrative. At which points in *Two Cars, One Night* would you suggest that the different phases begin and end?
2 How does *Two Cars, One Night* expand and contract time for the audience?
3 Christopher Vogler suggests, in his book *The Writer's Journey: Mythic Structures for Writers*, that there is a universal story form, which he calls the 'mythic structure'. He believes that stories follow a particular pattern, that central protagonists (whether male or female) follow the '12 steps of the hero's journey':

1. Ordinary world
2. Call to adventure
3. Refusal of the call
4. Meeting the mentor
5. Crossing the first threshold
6. Tests, allies, enemies
7. Approach to the inmost cave
8. Ordeal
9. Reward
10. Road back
11. Resurrection
12. Return with elixir

• To what extent is this formula true of *Two Cars, One Night*?
• In your opinion, are such patterns always true of short films?
• If films are indeed formulaic, where is the pleasure for audiences?

Page 1 of 1 — Short Films

1 page

worksheet **11** **Genre codes and conventions**

A genre has been defined as 'a style, variety or category, especially in art, film and literature' (the word's origin is French). One of the central ideas behind the study of films is that they can be approached by a process of categorisation. From the early days of film production, it was noticed that particular stories, set in certain times and locations, and with recognisable characters, were successful in drawing audiences into cinemas. Essentially, genres offered the means by which the industry sought to repeat and capitalise upon previous box-office success. Genre is not an unproblematic concept. Films are rarely 'generically pure'; they tend to refer to each other (intertextuality) and to other cultural and social events.

Genre as critical approach

In the late 1960s and 1970s, French critics started to develop the genre approach to film criticism. André Bazin argued that there is more to any genre than a mere list of codes and conventions, however. He expressed his belief that genres operate according to the structures of a universal and timeless code that he called myth.

Another critic, Christian Metz, suggested that part of the nature of genres is change. He looked at the Western and observed how it had gone through a cycle of changes over its history: from 'a classic stage, to a self-parody of the classics, to a period where films contest the position that they are part of a genre, and finally to a critique of the genre itself'.

Steve Neale in *Genre* (1991) suggests that genres should be seen as 'systems of orientations, expectations and conventions that circulate between industry, text and subject'.

Task

Look again at *Two Cars, One Night* and consider which genres it might be positioned within. How accurate would each of the following genres be as a category in which to place the film?

• Romance
• Comedy
• Teen movie
• Drama
• Social realist picture

Page 1 of 1 — Short Films

1 page

To more fully consider the mode of representation of the characters within *Two Cars, One Night*, see **Worksheet 12**.

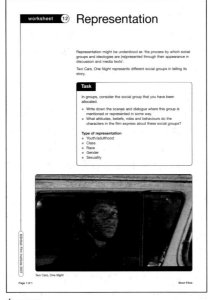

worksheet **12** **Representation**

Representation might be understood as 'the process by which social groups and ideologies are (re)presented through their appearance in discussion and media texts'.

Two Cars, One Night represents different social groups in telling its story.

Task

In groups, consider the social group that you have been allocated.

• Write down the scenes and dialogue where this group is mentioned or represented in some way.
• What attitudes, beliefs, roles and behaviours do the characters in the film express about these social groups?

Type of representation
• Youth/adulthood
• Class
• Race
• Gender
• Sexuality

Two Cars, One Night

Page 1 of 1 — Short Films

1 page

To access student worksheets and other online materials go to *Teaching Short Films* at **www.bfi.org.uk/tfms** and enter User name: **shorts@bfi.org.uk** and Password: **te1203sf**.

A shot towards the midpoint of the film sees an elderly male Maori address Polly, the girl, with a greeting: '*Kia-Ora*' (hello). She winds up the window, maybe remembering parental advice to not talk to strange men. This is the only time that an adult speaks directly to a child within the film – perhaps this is a comment on the generation gap.

Production

Two Cars, One Night was supported by state funds from the New Zealand Film Commission. The NZFC was established in 1978 by an Act of the New Zealand Parliament and has the statutory responsibility *'to encourage and participate and assist in the making, promotion, distribution and exhibition of films made in New Zealand by New Zealanders on New Zealand subjects'*. It provides loans and equity financing to assist in the development and production of feature films and short films, though it does not itself produce films. The Film Commission is also active in the sales and marketing of films and assists with training and professional development in the industry. Since its foundation, indigenous filmmaking has become very popular: *Once Were Warriors* (Lee Tamahori, New Zealand, 1994) and *Whale Rider* (Niko Caro, New Zealand, 2002) were both international hits that drew on the folk traditions and mythical storytelling of the Maori. By being nominated for an Oscar in 2004 for Best Short Film (Live Action), *Two Cars, One Night* is further testimony to how the state subsidy of films can develop a sustainable film industry. New Zealand also has provided the locations and crews for a number of international blockbusters, including *The Lord of the Rings* trilogy (all Peter Jackson, New Zealand, 2001–3) and *King Kong* (Peter Jackson, New Zealand, 2005). To explore more fully with your class aspects of the short film industry at home and abroad, have the students complete the reading and task on **Worksheet 13**.

Representation

One sequence towards the middle of the film involving a car and a tattoed, muscular Maori, seems to comment on how male aspirations are formed in contemporary culture. Cars are seen as status symbols in many societies and it is no different in these children's world. When a nice car pulls away from the parking lot in slow motion, its engine growling powerfully, its driver, a man with the full-facial colouring of the Maori Ta Moko (tattoo), acknowledges Romeo with a slow nod of the head. Romeo's awe-filled whisper *'Sweet as ...'* makes it clear how much he looks up to this version of masculinity. The contemporary phenomenon of tattooing within Maori gang culture has been interpreted as an attempt to reclaim the social power that many feel has been lost since colonisation. The tattoo has a long history in Polynesia and Maoris were its key proponents:

> The Moko is similar to an identity card, or passport. For men, the Moko shows their rank, their status and their ferocity, or virility. The wearer's position of power and authority can be instantly recognized in his Moko. Certain other outward signs, combined with a particular Moko, could instantly define the 'identity card' of a person. For example, a chief with Moko and at the same time wearing a dog cloak could be identified as a person of authority, in charge of warriors. (www.history-nz.org/maori3.html)

Romeo is trying to make sense of manhood and masculinity. One aspect of his characterisation is revelaed through his speech. It includes the assimilation of adult ideas; he is clearly aping his elders without fully understanding the issues he pronounces upon. In his view homosexuality, for instance, is tied to notions of class 'You're allowed to be a gay when you're a lawyer, hey?'. The girl, Polly, has a much more matter-of-fact response, showing a fuller understanding of the issues 'Yes, my auntie's a gay … she's got a girlfriend'.

A close analysis of the film in terms of the representation of social class is revealing. Romeo and Polly display learned attitudes to the trappings of wealth, for example, in their discussion of the value of Polly's fake diamond ring. This ring, which Polly reveals is not real towards the end of the film, acts as a symbol on several levels: it carries connotations of aspirations to wealth, and of commitment and marriage. However, it is as also a simple gift from one child to another that marks the momentic of a significant moment of human interaction. The final sequence uses slow motion in order to heighten the dramatic importance of these final moments. Viewers are left with a sense of the importance of this formative moment for the main protagonist, Romeo.

Case study 3: The short film industry

This case study focuses on representative institutions and organisations that comprise the short film industry. Most Media and Film Studies students look forward to the opportunity of producing their own films. With this in mind, the activities in this case study aim to develop the knowledge, understanding and skills that will form a foundation for practical production. This case study is supported by a range of handouts and additional materials, which can be accessed as part of the online materials at www.bfi.org.uk/tfms. **Worksheets 13 and 14** provide an overview of the short film industry and offer a solid base of knowledge and understanding for practical work. These worksheets are grounded in research tasks, but also provide an opportunity for creative thinking and imagination.

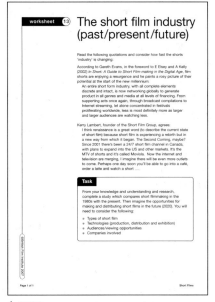

1 page

This case study broadly covers the following areas:

- Development
- Production
- Distribution
- Exhibition
- Marketing
- Vocations.

1 of 7 pages

For each of these short film industry areas teachers will find general information to help them to develop their own knowledge and under-standing and inform their lesson planning activities for their lessons. Following this are case studies of professional organisations, companies or individuals. These take various forms, such as summaries or over-views of information and original interviews. The resources section provides further examples of professional organisations and companies for each of these short film industry areas. These might be useful to students developing their knowledge and understanding of the industry.

● Development

There are several aspects to the developmental stages of a short film and advice on each of these is available from a number of sources. It is often said that '*a film is only as good as its story*' and while this may be accurate, the way in which that story is told is also key to its success. For this reason, the research and development stages of professional media products frequently account for more than half the time taken to bring the short film from initial idea to actual completion. Many short films have extended gestation periods where their treatments (production overview documents that include directions to camera and script information) are reworked and repositioned to meet the demands of possible investors.

The Script Factory

The Script Factory states on its website (www.scriptfactory.co.uk/) that it exists to '*fill the gap between writers and the industry*'. It offers script training for writers, both in the UK and abroad. Following the old maxim that '*all writing is rewriting*', the Script Factory offers a script development service to newcomers and professionals. It stages masterclasses where filmmakers and actors showcase new writing. The Script Factory also edits and manages the UK Screenwriters Network, a daily email digest for writers, in partnership with Shooting People. The Script Factory currently runs a range of training programmes in partnership with the National Film and Television School's Short Course Unit, under the banner The NFTS Short Course Factory.

First Light

First Light funds and inspires the making of short films by young people in the UK that reflect the diversity of their lives. It has already enabled over 9,000 young people between the ages of five and 18 to write, act, shoot and produce over 600 films. Working with filmmakers and industry organisations, First Light films cover many topics and genres, and make use of accessible digital film technology. First Light has established partnerships across the country and provide trainers, equipment and an understanding of the processes of film production to youth and community organisations, as well as maintaining a presence at festivals and short film events.

● Production companies

Numerous production companies specialise in short film. Given the extensive costs associated with professional film production, it is increasingly rare for companies to concentrate solely on the production of short films – it is much more likely that short film production will be one aspect of a slate of productions for a variety of markets – in advertising, music video and documentary production, for instance. **Worksheet 15** considers three short films that received single releases and should be researched by students to make them aware of the limitations and potentials of the short film as a marketable commodity.

worksheet 15 Single short film releases

There have been very few commercial releases of single short films; they are much more usually released in compilations of about 10 films. If we compare this with the music industry, it would be like only compilation albums being released and no singles.

A few notable exceptions are:

● *Rubber Johnny* (Chris Cunningham, UK, 2005) – an experimental arthouse film released with an accompanying photographic book.
● *Scummy Man* (Paul Fraser, UK, 2006) – a short film inspired by the song 'When the Sun Goes Down' by the Arctic Monkeys.
● *My Wrongs #8245–8249 & 117* (Chris Morris, UK, 2002) – a comedy short by Chris Morris.

There is clearly a potential market for single short films, which has yet to be fully exploited.

Task

1 Conduct a web search on each of the short films named above and suggest reasons why they were selected for individual release.
2 Research the potential market for short films by conducting a questionnaire survey. Try to establish who might buy new short films and what they would be looking for in a product of this type.
3 Choose one of the short films that you have studied on your course and decide how to promote it to an audience. You will need to make decisions about the following:
● Company name
● Product art design
● Profile of typical consumer
● Outlets for the product

1 page

Silver Films

Silver Films is one example of numerous innovative companies that have forged a reputation for producing high-quality short films. Silver Films has produced four short films todate: *Jump* (Simon Fellows, UK, 2001), *About a Girl, Talking with Angels* (Yousaf Ali Khan, UK, 2003) and *Endgame* (Gary Wicks, UK, 2001), and has established itself as a leading small company within the sector. The company's managing director, Janey de Nordwall, sees a market in the production of advertisements (primarily for the games industry and television), short films and feature-length movies. The following are excerpts from an interview in summer 2006:

Q. I believe that Silver Films is now ten years old. Can you outline its history?

It was originally based up in Manchester but is now based in London. It started out producing commercials for the games industry and organising large live events and product launches. It was very successful in its first phase, making lots of money and was lots of fun but I always knew that I wanted to produce films and when I had a particularly poor millennium I had a 'mid-career crisis' where I thought about what I really wanted from life. I'd been prudent enough with the money to be able to take a year off from the hectic schedule of commercials work for a research and development phase where I investigated changing the direction of the company: working out how to move from commercials into feature film. I was conscious that moving from thirty-second commercials to ninety-minute feature films is quite a leap so short films really appealed as a means to learn the role of the film producer. I also liked the idea of working with teams of people over time rather than just making an on/off film; I like the idea of developing new talent. I wanted to test the market in a low-risk way; all products have to go in to test whatever the business. There are so many one-off short films, but I wanted to get together a portfolio of projects for investors to buy in to. I had been working with some really good writers and directors who were experienced in their fields but who hadn't ever done feature films before. I decided to make some short films with these directors in particular and to then move into features with them, so I had to know that these people had feature projects in mind and ready for me to option.

Q. How have you been able to finance your short films?

In the first four years of Silver Films I turned over a million pounds, so when I approached Business Angels, a network of venture capitalists who invest in businesses through the Enterprise Investment Scheme, they knew that I was someone who could make things happen and sell ideas. The EIS allows tax relief and relief on capital gains at the end of a five-year period of investment, so it's a good way of establishing creative partnerships. Other producers had told me that it wouldn't ever work because it's so hard to get investment into individual short films but here they are investing in my company, and that makes quite a difference, as I'm matching their investment with my own money and experience. It was still very scary pitching to a group of unsmiling grey suits, but my dad come along with me and kept telling me to smile from the back of the room!'

Q. Where is Silver Films heading at the present time?
The company now has an option on a book by Stuart David (of Belle and Sebastian) called 'Nalda Said', which is being developed into a screenplay for our first full-length production. Silver Films still has its original investors who continue to support my vision and the company's direction. We've recently converted some development loans into equity in order to raise further funds to put directly into the development of 'Nalda Said'. The first draft is expected by the end of this year.

Q. In what ways are your short films finding audiences?
What is surprising is that my films have a life beyond that I'd expected. I'm still having people contact me six years after 'About a Girl' was made saying that they've just seen it in a festival and do I have time to answer a few questions... That's what filmmaking is about for me.

Q. In what ways do you think that new technologies are affecting the production and distribution of short films?
I'm very interested in new forms of communication; in how audiences can be reached through more innovative ways of selling rather than 'buy three for the price of two!'. My ongoing work in commercials and with the games industry has made me aware of the speed of change and needing to stay informed about audiences and innovations.

Janey de Nordwall discusses her work as an independent producer more fully later in this chapter.

● Exhibition

Securing the theatrical exhibition of short films is virtually impossible in today's mainstream cinemas. Film festivals and specialist screenings are likely to be the only occasions when short films make it to the big screen. Short filmmakers are therefore becoming increasingly proactive in developing innovative platforms to ensure that their films reach audiences. **Worksheet 16** requires students to complete textual analysis exercises in order to make them familiar with the growing

1 page

range of companies that work with the short film form in production, exhibition and distribution contexts. Private companies and national broadcasting organisations have also developed online portals in attempts to secure audiences:

Atom Films

Atom Films was the pioneer of streaming digital video through the World Wide Web and was founded in 1999. Within a year of its launch this company had one million users and targeted the new techno-savvy generation. Spike Jonze, short-film maker and video artist, joined the board as adviser in that same year. The company has developed a profile as an aggressive and forward-thinking enterprise with the ability to create new markets. Atom Films now delivers short-film comedies, animations and dramas to more than five million people each month. Atom Films is the leading next generation entertainment company and claims, on the home page of its website, to have *'redefined the way entertainment was created, distributed, marketed and consumed'*; first in America and then globally. Indeed, Atom Films now has the largest available catalogue of short films and has established a strong relationship with independent filmmakers and animators. Atom Films markets and distributes high-quality short form entertainment to more than 100 partners and to audiences worldwide, with significant presence on major Internet sites, broadband services, television, airlines, home-entertainment companies, as well as hand-held and wireless devices. The Atom Films website (www.atomfilms.com) is consistently ranked among Media Metrix's top 20 entertainment sites. Atom Films was the first company to transmit to hand-held PDA devices in America. The Press Cuttings on its website offer a fascinating insight in to a dotcom business that has been very successful – not least because of its aggressive business strategies and buying in to film production and sponsoring new modes of production. It has also built successful partnerships with a film industry that felt threatened by the growth of cable television:

> Short-form entertainment has always been a favourite of audiences; but the economics of entertainment distribution have shut it out of the mainstream and restricted the format to 'niche' outlets. The emergence of new delivery platforms, especially the internet, is fuelling the emergence of short-form entertainment as a viable business; and causing even mainstream outlets, like cable, to revisit the use of short-form entertainment to retain audiences,' says Jim Banister, Executive Vice President of Warner Bros. Online.

Atom Films has formed alliances with a range of major media companies interested in making their catalogue of short films available to global audiences. Atom's distribution partners and customers include HBO, @Home, Go Network/Infoseek, Sundance Channel, Warner Bros. Online, Continental Airlines, Air Canada, RealNetworks, Reel.com, Mr. Showbiz, Broadcast DVD, Film.com, College Broadcast Network, Air New Zealand and SonicNet. The company is also working with national bodies, such as the American Film Institute, Australian

Film Commission and Norwegian Film Institute, which are seeking to showcase emerging talent and promote their countries as sites of production. '*The time for bringing short films and animation to mainstream audiences is now*,' says Jeff Schwager, executive producer of Go Entertainment.

In 2004, Atom Films established a partnership with Customflix that made award-winning shorts available on custom-made compilation DVDs. These are mailed out to customers who have perused the online collection and placed an order. It also inked deals with AOL, Singingfish and Blinkx for short film distribution and these agreements helped to fuel Atom Films' soaring online advertiser growth.

BBC Film Network

The BBC's Film Network offers a selection of short films as high resolution downloads in full screen, near-DVD quality. If you subscribe (it is free) you will automatically receive three of Film Network's very best shorts every fortnight, downloaded in the background and ready for you to watch. Each short is available to watch for 28 days and is automatically deleted after that period. If you don't subscribe, you may select shorts to download yourself. All the films on Film Network are offered via streaming. The advantages of streaming are that the film plays immediately and, because the film doesn't end up on the user's computer, there are no rights issues and so films can be offered for a long period of time. However, the video is small and, because the file is compressed, the quality of the image isn't great. Also, if your connection to the web becomes busy, your viewing may be interrupted.

By offering films as a download, however, Film Network doesn't need to compress the files so it can offer films full screen, in a similar quality to DVD. The disadvantage of downloads is that you have to wait for the file to download and the file ends up on the user's computer. Film Network gets around this by offering subscriptions where files are automatically downloaded in the background, which means that you don't have to wait and by using digital rights management the BBC can restrict how long users can use the file on their computer.

The hi-resolution downloads were offered as a public trial for 12 months, until April 2007. The BBC used the trial to test how the improved viewing experience affects audience behaviour and how people consume short films in this way. It also needed to assess the possible market impact of providing short films as hi-resolution downloads and if the benefits to the public outweighed any possible negative impact upon commercial services. There are also rights holders who need to be assured that the digital rights management technology is secure. At the end of the trial Film Network hopes to continue offering short films as hi-resolution downloads and will endeavour to provide existing users with a seamless transition to the continuing offer.

Worksheet 20 is a practical exercise that requires students to plan a season of short films and make judgments about how to secure audiences for the exhibition of short films.

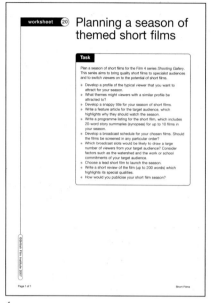

1 page   1 page

To access student worksheets and other online materials go to *Teaching Short Films* at **www.bfi.org.uk/tfms** and enter User name: **shorts@bfi.org.uk** and Password: **te1203sf.**

● Distribution

The vast majority of short films do not secure distribution deals, though there is a growing and profitable DVD compilation market for the very limited number of short films that achieve recognition or notoriety. To more fully explore the distribution and exhibition of short films with your class, see **Worksheet 17**.

Future Shorts

Future Shorts is the brainchild of entrepreneur Fabien Riggall, who realised that there is a strong interest in short film, but very few opportunities for those who are interested in the form to see public screenings:

> Outside of festivals there is nowhere to get short films seen by a real audience. The UK's pub scene helps small bands get their music heard by a diverse audience, but there's nothing like that for short film. Future Shorts set out to fill that void. (www.futureshorts.com).

Since its first screening in a pub in 2003, the Future Shorts network has grown to include more than thirty venues, which regularly screen programmes of short films. Regular screenings are now programmed in capital cities such as London, Paris and Madrid, but also there also regional events at venues such as Cornwall and Colchester. Future Shorts also draws audiences when it organises abroad – from Canada to Latvia. Future Shorts finds ways of making screenings quirky and original events in order to ensure an audience; for instance, it recently ran a programme called 'Dive-in' movies at Tooting Bec Lido. Future Shorts also has a presence at film and music festivals:

> When we did Glastonbury we had about 2000 people a day through the tent. That's the joy of festivals – people just want to explore and look at new things. (Fabien Riggall, Future Shorts' media pack)

Future Shorts, like many new business ventures, needs to cultivate an audience over time if it is to be successful in the long run. Fabien Rigall is clear about the need to overcome viewers' prejudices about the short film form:

> The Future Shorts' network was established to create a fully independent exhibition and distribution network where short film can be recognised as a medium in its own right. The Future Shorts' brand stands for quality, innovation and the recognition of new talent. Future Shorts is committed to making short film more accessible and to altering audiences' perceptions of the short film medium.

Audiences for Future Shorts screenings are around 2000 each month, many of whom are looking for an alternative to the multiplex culture of Hollywood glam and little substance. The organisation 'acts as a filter, exposing audiences to a unique quality slate of films', including fiction, animation, documentary, music video and experimental film. So, Future Shorts has set up a number of strategic partnerships in order to source short films that will satisfy the appetites of their audiences. One of these is with Kodak, which runs a short film showcase in association with BAFTA every six months. 'There's a whole short film culture, especially in London', says Dan Clark, Kodak's Emerging Films Manager. 'It's quite trendy to do short films now.' Fabien Riggall says that he is constantly seeking new quality films to add to the Future Shorts' programme, and here 'quality' is a subjective judgment rather than relating to the specific technical demands and production values of broadcast programming:

> There are no real criteria for the films I programme. If I like it, I put it in. Curating films is like making a mix-tape – you have to understand your audience and ensure diversity of material. Regardless of the budget or names involved. We just want to show films that work within the medium. It doesn't matter if the camera's a bit shaky and it was made on DV for £50, if a film tells a story and is well acted and directed, then it's achieved its status. (Future Shorts' media pack)

In addition to the screenings, Future Shorts sets out to provide a link between emerging talent and the industry by acting as consultants for *The Reel*, a monthly shorts compilation sent out to advertising agencies and production companies. Future Shorts has recently ventured into selling short films directly to its audience by establishing its own short film label. It markets these releases as limited editions in much the same way that the music industry used to promote its records, rendering the products desirable because of their exclusivity and limited number.

The industry is starting to recognise the value of short film, moving on from the perception that shorts are solely research-and-development mechanisims for finding new talent. Since the filmmaking technologies are moving so quickly there is a growing interest in the commercial aspect, as Riggall suggests:

> Whether it's mobile phones or broadband, these technologies need content and I think that is where shorts can work very well. It's not likely to be immediate, but once there is an audience and people are aware of the short film medium, there's no reason why short films can't be as sexy as music videos. (Future Shorts' media pack)

● Marketing

Since short films are rarely distributed theatrically they are rarely marketed in the same way as feature films. Essentially, the role of marketing companies is to create and produce publicity material, which is intended to prompt and encourage cinemagoers to attend screenings and to maximise the profitability of the film product. While short film is unlikely to be promoted in the same way as feature film, it is increasingly common for short filmmakers to consider the ways in which they can create an image for their films and attract an audience. Short films are not typically seen as conventional media products and therefore not sold directly to consumers, though some individual short films are now being positioned in the marketplace – either through their associations with television personalities, such as Chris Morris, or the music industry, such as *Scummy Man* and the Arctic Monkeys. Notwithstanding such exceptions, the most viable way of securing an audience for a short film is by submitting it to one of the burgeoning number of film festivals (see the list in the final section of this guide).

Brief Encounters/Encounters Film Festival, Bristol

Brief Encounters is Bristol's annual celebration of the short film and is the leading competitive short film festival in the UK. It combines extensive film exhibition, including premières and new talent from all over the globe, with education and training from respected industry professionals and an array of special events and parties. The first Brief Encounters festival of short film took place in 1995. It was originally seen as a one-off, part of the international celebrations marking the centenary of cinema. But it proved so successful that it started to attract major levels of sponsorship from companies and organisations impressd by its 'talent parade' of short filmmakers. Since its launch Brief Encounters has not only consistently showcased a wide range of shorts, but has also presented a full programme of special events that have featured key industry figures such as Anthony Minghella, Shane Meadows and Alan Yentob. The Encounters Festival now comprises Brief Encounters and Animated Encounters, now in its fifth year, the UK's leading annual festival of animated film, dedicated to celebrating the diverse world of animation with screenings, seminars, masterclasses and parties. Animated Encounters is an international meeting place and aims to stimulate, inspire and entertain the industry and the public. The Festival's increased international stature is demonstrated by the fact that it is now the nominated British festival for the prestigious European Cartoon D'Or.

Raindance Film Festival, London

Raindance is a foundation that has been dedicated to fostering and promoting independent film in the UK and around the world since 1992. The foundation combines the Raindance Film Festival, Raindance Kids Film Festival, Raindance Film Productions and training courses and claims to be 'the voice of Independent film in Britain'. Raindance hosts the prestigious British Independent Film Awards in London, which spans the full spectrum of the art, craft and business of independent movies – from guerrilla-style low- or no-budget productions to big-budget independent blockbusters. Created in 1998, the British Independent Film Awards sets out to celebrate merit and achievement in independently funded British filmmaking, to honour new talent, and to promote British films and filmmaking to a wider public. Training courses are at the heart of the Raindance structure, aiming to give individuals the tools to start shooting their film. They combine traditional filmmaking approaches with new digital technology, and have an annual interaction with over 3,000 filmmakers – writers, directors, producers, actors, agents and Film and Media students.

To more fully explore short film festivals and their impact on those working with the short film form, see **Worksheets 18 and 19**.

Marketing student films

Student filmmakers should also consider the extent to which they can market their short films as media products. The best time to do this is in the pre-production and post-production phases. Use **Worksheet 21** 'Getting Your Short Film Shown', from *Media Magazine* no 16, to encourage learners to consider their films as products throughout their practical work. Students should also be encouraged to research new and emerging ways of securing an audience for their films over the web. **Worksheet 22** provides research activities to develop knowledge and understanding and offers advice on how to submit films to web-cinemas. **Worksheet 23** encourages students to work collaboratively in preparing press releases for their short films, with an example from the featured student production *Morning After, Night Before* (Sarah Ellis, UK, 2005).

1 of 3 pages

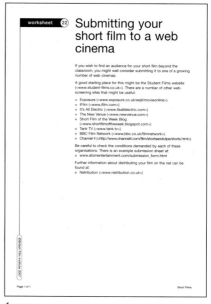

1 page

1 page

● Vocations

The number of differing roles that fall within the short film industry is extensive and students will benefit from understanding how these roles relate to each other, particularly within the context of their own practical productions where they are likely to have experience of several roles each.

The role of the producer: Janey de Nordwall

Janey de Nordwall is a BAFTA-winning producer and director of her own media production company Silver Films. The excerpts are from an original interview with the author in August 2006. Janey went to school in south Manchester and then studied for a BTEC qualification in Business Studies at college, though she remains adamant that neither of these experiences really prepared her for the job that she now does:

> Good producers haven't been taught a trade as such; they're people who balance a critical approach to their work with a creative attitude to solving problems. You have to trust your own instinct and judgements and be prepared to have an opinion.

Janey worked in a number of roles that allowed her to develop an understanding of how the television and film industries work 'from the inside', before setting up her own business, Silver Films, in 1996; for instance she worked at the Granada studio tour in the chromakey room where tourists are superimposed on the set of the Rovers' Return! This may not have provided any great technical insights into production, but it meant that she could develop the communication skills on which she now relies – deftly setting clients and creatives at ease and getting on with the job of filmmaking. Janey also worked as a receptionist at a post-production facility called Editz, but soon realised that she wanted to *'be in on the film-production act much earlier'*, so she cold-called clients, asking for work in production. On learning that production posts were only available on a freelance basis, Janey set herself up as a production co-ordinator.

> For me, the Enterprise Allowance scheme was brilliant! Critics of this government-funded scheme have suggested that it was merely a way of getting young people off the dole queue; however, it allowed me to make my own decisions. That was an important thing for me to discover – that I could make my own decisions.

Janey next worked on pop promos and music videos in the thriving Manchester music scene, gaining experience of the roles involved in any professional production:

> It was all very low-budget and, in production, everyone does everything and makes it up as they go along, so that laid a real foundation – I got to see how each different role fits together to produce an outcome.

After working in research for television shows for Channel 4 and Granada, Janey took a job in a production company making commercials where she met Brian Percival, who was later to direct *About a Girl*. She learned about the production industry: working on film, co-ordinating big crews; watching other producers; seeing how to keep a production to budget and on schedule. After a year she went freelance as a TV producer in an advertising company before setting up Silver Films in 1996.

Q. Did you study the media at all at school?

Media and Film Studies weren't an option in my day, so I never considered working in film as a real possibility. I do remember watching a behind-the-scenes documentary on *Indiana Jones and the Temple of Doom* when I was 13 and being excited by the work of the film crew rather than the glamour of the cast. I have dyslexia, though this wasn't recognised at that time, so my teachers thought that I was stupid and lazy and wouldn't amount to much! Actually, being dyslexic has a positive side: I find scripts easier to read than books and tend to be able to see the wood rather than the trees, which helps me to troubleshoot quickly and efficiently.

Q. How would you define your job as a producer?

One of the big mistakes that are made when it comes to understanding the role of producer is in failing to distinguish between producers and production managers. Producers make the whole production happen and production managers only work the budget and schedule. Where producers are on the project right from the start and stay with the film throughout its life, production managers are employed to ensure that the production of a film remains on track only after it enters the actual production phase. Since production managers aren't involved in generating the money for a film they rarely have the same say in how the production runs. Producers greenlight productions, secure funding to the point of completion and establish the budget for the production. But more than this, they are the people who make things happen and ensure that the job gets done, so they need to solve problems and overcome obstacles on the ground.

Q. How do you choose which scripts to commission?

When I read a script I think visually and create my own mental images from the words. I can't create these out of poor writing because the flaws get in the way but I can appreciate the good in something and have the ability to take that forward. So when I read a script I have to be able to visualise everything and then to make sure that I'm coming from the same angle as the director – I like that triangle of creativity between scriptwriter, director and producer. Filmmaking is about a team, NOT just about a director, though it's usually that director who receives the plaudits.

Q. So who actually owns the rights to a short film?

Short films should be treated like mini feature films. Contracts are drawn up during the early stages of a production to outline who owns what; who is responsible for what and who (if anyone) gets paid. Short films don't make money as a rule, so they are frequently a labour of love or a stepping-stone to a bigger project. You can't invest in anyone making a feature film if they haven't made short films or don't understand the industry. The actual ownership of short films is frequently a contested matter. A cinematographer would argue that he/she owns the images in that he/she created them, technically and artistically speaking; a director would claim ownership on the grounds that he/she had the vision to realise them; and a scriptwriter would argue that he/she was the originator of the ideas behind the images. That's a debate that goes on and on, and it's advisable that those discussions happen before the film goes into production. My experience has taught me, and I've been burned quite a few times, that it's important to have everything tied up in a contract, so that all parties are clear about where their rights and responsibilities lie.

Q. What was the exact nature of your role in making *About a Girl*?
Well, I was the producer of the film and my involvement started with reading the script and thinking 'Oh my God we have to make this film!' I was involved in the entire process: fundraising, pre-production, the shoot, post production, festival entry and sales and promotion of the film and, finally, collecting the BAFTA with the director, writer and actor of the film!
The script was unusual as we shot the second draft. However, we were advised not to make it by several industry people who said that it wouldn't do us any good as a first short as it wasn't really a 'film' and that we should focus on making a comedy! Belief in the script and the team convinced me to invest £30,000 into its production. Ten days before production, MIDA (now the North West Development Agency) matched this investment.

As a timescale, I read the script in January 2000 and started securing the funding from late April. By August I had all the money in so we went into pre-production in September and actually shot over a week in January. *About a Girl* was the first ever short film to be completely digitally post-produced. The film's budget had been set at £30,000 but it eventually ran to nearer to £35,000 because of the costs associated with buying the clearance rights to music – Britney Spears doesn't come cheap!

Q. Since you are from Manchester and two of your films are set there (*About a Girl* and *Talking with Angels*), do you feel any sort of social responsibility towards representing the community from which you sprang when it comes to making films?
No, not particularly! I don't even see myself as a British filmmaker, just a filmmaker. I'm more interested in making films with great stories and characters that evoke an emotional reaction from audiences. I'm also happy to locate a film wherever's right for the film. If the best place to set and produce a film is abroad then that's fine – we'll go there to make it. I do think you have to stay true to the integrity of the film, rather than making decisions based on finance. This may be hard to do but it's essential if you are to make the film that you set out to make.

Q. How important are festivals in getting the films known?

Film festivals are essential to the success of short films as awards ensure that they find an audience and the publicity, which seems such a great challenge to overcome for British filmmakers of all kinds. Our films are still being shown widely and it's pleasing that our efforts are being recognised. I've been lucky enough to follow the films abroad, America, Cannes, etc. and people should understand that both a producer and a director need to be prepared to talk about a film with energy and passion to make it successful. It's not over just because it's in the can. Having a strategy for festivals is essential – it's not necessarily about blanket coverage but more about knowing what is best for the film. *Talking with Angels* was entered into about 60 festivals in order to get it widely known, but *About a Girl* went into prestige festivals like Edinburgh, London and Manchester and, of course, we were awarded the BAFTA for that short film.

Q. Is it possible to make a living solely from short filmmaking?

It's hard to earn a living making feature films. It's impossible to make a living just making short films so it's important to secure another income. My business requires me to keep the money coming in so I've done a lot of work of varying kinds in order to keep a cashflow through the company. If you are creative, and you want to work in the creative world, you need to earn a living somehow – to allow yourself to be creative. Unfortunately, however, the creative world rarely offers much pay, so you need to find an income to give you freedom to be creative.

Q. What advice would you offer to a young person who wanted to become a producer and businesswoman like yourself?

Well, firstly I see myself in terms of what I do rather than as a woman doing what I do. I haven't encountered any sexism in the job, I'm glad to say. As for advice I'd say 'take your time'. Experience is invaluable for a producer as it teaches you how to deal with people and situations, and how to troubleshoot effectively. It's taken me 15 years to get this far and I'm still learning and growing. Be honest and true to your values and convictions and treat everyone how you'd like to be treated. Very simple advice really.

Throughout this interview Janey showed that she is very level-headed about what she expects from the short film industry and recognises 'its unique potential to disappoint' as she has seen so many productions fail. Many more films are commissioned than ever find an audience, and it is only Janey's energy and determination to see her films through that have made them successful.

Case Study 4: Short film practical production

The natural development of any study of short films is likely to be the production of student-produced texts that illustrate the basic conventions of short film. Since most of the short film practical production work undertaken in post-16 settings is based on live-action drama this case study is on this form. Centres wishing to develop alternative forms of short film production, such as animation, advertisements or music video can amend the processes accordingly. The following case study is designed to supply teachers with a clear model for teaching the development and production of short films and broadly covers the following areas:

- Pre-production
- Production
- Post production
- Reflection, assessment and evaluation.

This case study is conceived as an overview of how teachers might effectively manage practical production work and avoid common pratfalls, rather than being a step-by-step guide for students. Pete Fraser and Barney Oram's *Teaching Digital Video Production* (BFI) offers fuller advice and technical detail in this regard. This section should be read in parallel with Scheme of Work 4, so that the activities and screenings are developmental. This case study focuses in depth on a representative student production, *Morning After, Night Before* (Sarah Ellis, UK, 2005), available on the BFI website at www.bfi.org.uk/tfms/shortfilms. It is supported by a range of handouts and additional materials, including students' planning notes from the three phases of the production. These can be also accessed at www.bfi.org.uk/tfms/shortfilms.

● The *unofficial* rules of practical production

Wherever possible, *constrain* the production work that students are set – particularly in the early stages of the course. It is better to start simply and further develop projects at a later stage than for students to fail to complete over-ambitious short films. In any case, some of the most successful short films are developed from strong ideas founded on a simple premise. Consider:
- Restricting the number of characters
- Limiting the quantity of locations and ensuring easy accessibility
- Assessing the complexity of lighting requirements
- Employing minimal dialogue
- Addressing difficulties of shooting at different times of day and night
- Assessing sound-recording issues
- Reducing the number of crew needed
- Issuing shot recipes / transition recipes, which state (and limit) requirements, thus 'forcing the students' creativity' through problem-solving.

It is also helpful to build students' knowledge, understanding and skills gradually, developing their confidence through the increasing sophistication of the set tasks they need to undertake before assessment.

● Verse into light project (micro shorts)

This project is designed to produce short films in the most technically straightforward of ways. It is conceived as an introduction to the digital technologies that will support learning throughout a course and allows students to get 'hands-on' experience at an early stage. The project builds on students' understanding of the pop video form and allows them to see a project through the three-tiered production process and to reflect on the nature of collaborative group work and the quality of the final outcomes.

Verse into light task for students

In small groups, produce a film poem of no more than one minute in length. The reading of this poem will form the soundtrack that you will 'cut' images against in the editing suite. There will be *no more than six edits* in your film poem. Your group will be issued with a camera to shoot these images and you are allowed only two 'takes' of each shot so make sure that you have rehearsed each shot thoroughly before shooting. The content of these shots is entirely up to you – the object of the exercise is to be creative within the constraints of the project!

● The three-tiered production process

Practical production work is best approached through a clear understanding of the stages of production:

- Pre-production (planning and development)
- Production (shooting, sound-recording and editing)
- Post-production (product testing, marketing, distribution, evaluation).

Students should form production teams from which both cast and crew are drawn and should meet regularly to ensure that they are on schedule. Broadly, it is helpful to plan a 40% (pre-production), 30% (production) and 30% (post production) time-split for each of the phases, as the pre-production work is typically more time-consuming and teachers frequently supplement this phase with discussion of examples and models of successful work. Emphasise the importance of the pre-production phase as this forms the foundation for the entire production.

Pre-production tasks

Worksheets 24a–27 provide a range of activities to initiate practical production work and establish a solid foundation of knowledge and understanding. Since the quality of pre-production materials will determine the overall standard, these worksheets have been designed to provide a sense of progression and development.

Working from models

Students should be familiar with a variety of short films prior to commencing their own projects and be able to display an understanding of the form and content of short films. Presentations of past work by students from the preceding year will give younger learners insights into the practical production process. Within A Level courses this is likely to be A2 students presenting to AS students. Ensure that this is a two-way process for both cohorts by building a market-research aspect into the task set for the A2 students, and ask production teams to frame the presentations of their films around the three-tiered production process.

Setting realistic targets and managing expectations

Most of the short films students will view in the planning and research phases of their courses will be professionally produced with high production values. It is important that students have realistic perceptions of the work that they will produce and that they do not judge their own productions against short films that are produced by teams of experienced professionals using the latest technology. Students should understand that they will be assessed in relation to the extent of their learning within the project rather than solely on the quality of their final product.

Setting tasks and timescales

Breaking the three tiers of practical production into separate tasks and having the production teams draw up deadlines for each of these is essential to the successful completion of the project. **Worksheet 24a** provides a model of a production brief that can be used to establish parameters. Ensuring that there is time for the retrieval of some elements if things go wrong is crucial – the course of short filmmaking never does run smooth!

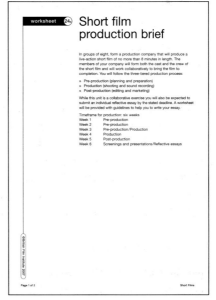

1 of 2 pages

To access student worksheets and other online materials go to *Teaching Short Films* at **www.bfi.org.uk/tfms** and enter User name: **shorts@bfi.org.uk** and Password: **te1203sf**.

Organising group work

Each group should appoint a producer to be the main point of contact with the teacher and the production team. Encouraging students to take responsibility for managing aspects of their own learning can be one of the learning outcomes against which they are assessed. Dividing up responsibilities is important if production teams are to work most efficiently. Not all learners will be able to have an equal contribution to all aspects of the short film production process, but there must be a degree of balance over the duration of the project. **Worksheet 24b** sets out the key production roles. These should be broken down so that students have a clear understanding of the tasks associated with each position. Screening *Living in Oblivion* will help to bring these roles to life.

If students are made aware of the time constraints under which they are working there is a greater likelihood that they will focus on each of the phases. **Worksheet 24c** provides a breakdown of the phases of short film development.

1 page

1 page

To access student worksheets and other online materials go to *Teaching Short Films* at **www.bfi.org.uk/tfms** and enter User name: **shorts@bfi.org.uk** and Password: **te1203sf**.

Worksheet 24d focuses students on the task of writing short films and suggests alternative processes for 'finding a strong story'.

Worksheet 25 moves learners towards the collaborative work of short film production. It sets out a 'synopsis' frame around which to structure the production. A model from *Morning After, Night Before* is included as an example.

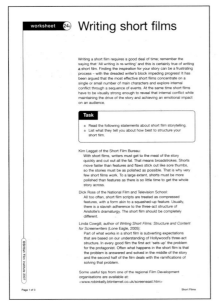

1 of 3 pages

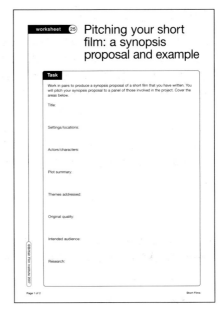

1 of 2 pages

1 page

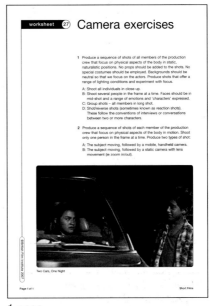

1 page

This activity is complemented by the characterisation work of **Worksheet 26** and a profile of one of the roles from the featured student production.

Before commencing their practical work, students should have the opportunity to put some of their theoretical learning (such as that in Schemes of work 1 and 2) into a practical context. **Worksheet 27** has been designed to ensure that students have had a chance to get 'hands-on' experience in a non-assessed context. Feedback from students shows that this activity can considerably enhance student understanding of effective shooting processes and the establishment of shared protocols during the actual production phase.

Production tasks

Worksheets 28 to 30 provide relevant information for this phase of the production. Where other guides in this series have taken a step-by-step approach to the production phase, these worksheets seek to provide overarching suggestions that will enhance the standard of student productions.

● Allowing students to work unsupervised
It is highly unlikely that any teacher will be able to supervise learners in all stages of the production – particularly when practical production work goes on location beyond the confines of the school or college premises. It is advisable to notify your colleagues if students are out of formal lessons in staff briefing meetings or through the school bulletin. Since the *in loco parentis* ruling requires a teacher to operate as a 'reasonable parent' might, it is important that colleagues within a department agree a policy for practical production that is shared with the senior leadership team (in much the same way that the drama department should have a policy for the extra-curricular activities of the school show). Ideally, parents should be informed of this policy and it should be publicised in the course materials.

Monitoring progress

It is essential that teachers maintain an active role in ensuring that the production work remains on track. Regular liaison with the producer of each short should be complemented with structured 'work-in-progress' presentations by students in scheduled production meetings attended by the entire team. Students should document each stage of the production process with a production diary or log.

Production codes

Worksheet 29 provides a model of a production code that was developed by a group of students to formalise their involvement within collaborative work. Students sign such a document in order to commit themselves to a contract for the duration of the project. Students benefit from developing their own production codes collaboratively rather than just signing up to one provided by a teacher, however, so this session might be led by a producer in order to systematise practical production work.

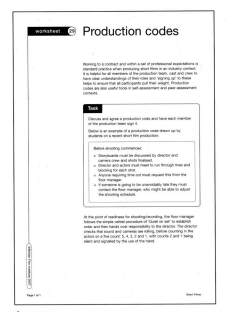

worksheet 29 — Production codes

Working to a contract and within a set of professional expectations is standard practice when producing short films in an industry context. It is helpful for all members of the production team, cast and crew to have clear understandings of their roles and 'signing up' to these helps to ensure that all participants pull their weight. Production codes are also useful tools in self-assessment and peer-assessment contexts.

Task

Discuss and agree a production code and have each member of the production team sign it.

Below is an example of a production code drawn up by students on a recent short film production:

Before shooting commences:
- Storyboards must be discussed by director and camera crew and shots finalised.
- Director and actors must meet to run through lines and blocking for each shot.
- Anyone requiring time out must request this from the floor manager.
- If someone is going to be unavoidably late they must contact the floor manager, who might be able to adjust the shooting schedule.

At the point of readiness for shooting/recording, the floor manager follows the simple verbal procedure of 'Quiet on set' to establish order and then hands over responsibility to the director. The director checks that sound and cameras are rolling, before counting in the actors on a five count: 5, 4, 3, 2 and 1, with counts 2 and 1 being silent and signalled by the use of the hand.

Page 1 of 1 — Short Films

1 page

worksheet 30 — Call sheet

This is an example of a call sheet from *Morning After, Night Before*. Use this format to create your own call sheet.

Thursday 6 November		Crew/Cast Required
AM	Character workshop / Scenes 1, 2a, 2b / View establishers/cutaways – reshoot as required	All / DoP/director / Sound engineer / Floor manager / Cast as called
2pm	Room X: Viewing rushes – reshoot as required / Transfer to edit suite	All / Editor
Friday 7 November		
8-9am	Library scenes 3, 4, 19, 19b, 20 / Floor manager	DoP/director
9 onwards	Scenes 5, 6, 7, 8, 12, 16	All actors
PM	Shoot, view, re-shoot as possible	DoP/director / Sound engineer / Floor manager / Actors as called
Late PM	Scenes 9, 10, 11 / Edit transfer	All actors / DoP/director / Editors
Monday 10 November		
10am	Scenes 13, 14	Cast for scenes / DoP/director / Sound engineer / Floor manager
PM	Edit transfer	Editors
Tuesday 11 November		
8-9am / 9 onwards	Scenes 15, 17 and scene catch-up / DoP/director	All cast standby
PM	Title sequence and credits/Edit transfer	2 x DoP/director/editors

Page 1 of 1 — Short Films

1 page

> To access student worksheets and other online materials go to *Teaching Short Films* at **www.bfi.org.uk/tfms** and enter User name: **shorts@bfi.org.uk** and Password: **te1203sf**.

Equipment rotas

Appointing a student to work alongside a technician (if your school enjoys this level of support – most do not) in ensuring that equipment is fairly distributed, can be a valuable learning experience in its own right. Teams are more likely to focus on using time productively if they are working within time constraints. School equipment insurance frequently requires equipment to be formally signed out when taken off site and, in any case, the formality of such a procedure should encourage students to adopt responsible attitudes to caring for the equipment. **Worksheet 30** is a model of a call sheet for *Night Before, Morning After*, which was used by those booking the equipment to ensure that each shoot had the technology required to be successful.

The soundtrack

Copyright and artistic property rights laws mean that if you want to use commercial music in your short film then you have to pay someone for the rights. Though it has been standard practice for teachers to allow students to use found material within their productions, this is effectively illegal if a short film is to be shown to an audience outside the school. Some digital editing packages now come with free looped music software (such as Soundtrack Pro) that is the aural equivalent of clipart. While this is one way of overcoming the copyright issue, it is more exciting to encourage students to create their own music to accompany their visuals. Another way that teachers have overcome the copyright issue is to source copyright-free music on library CDs or from websites that provide free music on the condition that the source is acknowledged in the closing credits. Students who wish to enter their films for festivals have to sign documents that prove that all music and images have gained copyright clearance.

Extra-curricular support

Drawing on support from colleagues in other departments can really enhance the learning experience of your students. Music departments frequently require their students to write and create original music and this might be used on the short film score to provide a real audience for the musicians' work. Drama departments can also provide guidance for the actors involved in productions. Where this is not possible, **Worksheet 28** has been designed to enhance the quality of student performances. Setting up a website for the department (Long Road Sixth Form College has a good example at www.longroadmedia.com) would be a fascinating project for the IT department and students following A Level computing courses. However, the reality of media teaching in many schools is that teachers work alone or with a small team and with limited resources. Local City Learning Centres have teams of specialist educators and more substantial resources that you can draw upon for the duration of the short film projects you plan for your students.

To access student worksheets and other online materials go to *Teaching Short Films* at **www.bfi.org.uk/tfms** and enter User name: **shorts@bfi.org.uk** and Password: **te1203sf**.

1 of 2 pages

Post-production tasks

To give students insights into how to enhance the quality of final versions of their own short films, **Worksheet 31** requires them to analyse the short film *Morning After, Night Before*. They will learn to make final revisions to a film prior to its completion for distribution or exhibition in certain contexts.

To access student worksheets and other online materials go to *Teaching Short Films* at **www.bfi.org.uk/tfms** and enter User name: **shorts@bfi.org.uk** and Password: **te1203sf**.

worksheet 31 Production: *Morning After, Night Before*

Production company simulation

Imagine that you work for an independent film production company, which has been commissioned by the BBC to develop a new series showcasing the work of up-and-coming filmmakers. A group of student filmmakers has submitted a 'rough cut' of *Morning After, Night Before* in the hope that it will be selected for broadcast. What advice would you offer to them on how to enhance their film in order to bring it to broadcast standard?

Task

Having watched the film as a class, divide into groups of four and elect a spokesperson to feed back ideas. You will have 30 minutes after a second viewing to discuss the film and form your responses.

Positive aspects	Suggestions for further development
Cinematography	
Locations	
Costume	
Soundtrack	
Script	
Casting/quality of acting	
Editing	
Any other areas	

1 page

Organising screening events

The standard of practical work at a centre will be driven up over time if students are able to learn from the successes of previous year groups. Encouraging students to take responsibility for organising screenings of their work will ensure that its status is raised within the cohort and within the institution. Inviting governors and senior leadership to events can ensure that your department is issued with the resources (both technical and human) in future years. Celebrating the successful realisation of practical production projects should be about more than just screening the films, however. Encourage students to deliver short presentations that summarise their learning and indicate the strengths and future learning targets stemming from their work.

Developing showreels and media packs

Increasingly, post-16 students are asked to produce portfolios of their work at interview for a place on Higher Education courses. Encourage them to develop showreels to represent their learning to admissions tutors. Media packs compile the promotional materials that are used to market films (and other media products) and are frequently aimed at potential advertisers or sponsors. Included in the BFI website for this guide are the samples from the *Morning After, Night Before* media pack. These illustrate the designer's intention to create a strong visual image for the film's promotional materials.

Reflection, evaluation and assessment

Developing reflective writing

Worksheet 32 encourages learners to structure their writing, as they did their practical production work, around the three-tiered production process. At the heart of good reflective writing is the ability to consider both the process of practical production and the quality of the final product *in terms of the learning* within the unit. Effective evaluative writing is certainly 'academic' in tone and students will need to be supported in developing the quality of their writing through a drafting process.

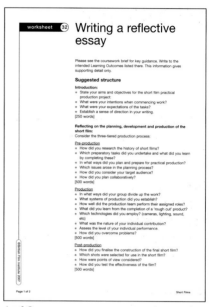

worksheet 32 **Writing a reflective essay**

Please see the coursework brief for key guidance. Write to the intended Learning Outcomes listed there. This information gives supporting detail only.

Suggested structure

Introduction:
- State your aims and objectives for the short film practical production project.
- What were your intentions when commencing work?
- What were your expectations of the tasks?
- Establish a sense of direction in your writing.
[250 words]

Reflecting on the planning, development and production of the short film:
Consider the three-tiered production process:

Pre-production
- How did you research the history of short films?
- Which preparatory tasks did you undertake and what did you learn by completing these?
- In what ways did you plan and prepare for practical production?
- Which issues arose in the planning process?
- How did you consider your target audience?
- How did you plan collaboratively?
[500 words]

Production
- In what ways did your group divide up the work?
- What systems of production did you establish?
- How well did the production team perform their assigned roles?
- What did you learn from the completion of a 'rough cut' product?
- Which technologies did you employ? (cameras, lighting, sound, etc)
- What was the nature of your individual contribution?
- Assess the level of your individual performance.
- How did you overcome problems?
[500 words]

Post-production
- How did you finalise the construction of the final short film?
- Which shots were selected for use in the short film?
- How were points of view considered?
- How did you test the effectiveness of the film?
[500 words]

Page 1 of 2   Short Films

1 of 2 pages

To access student worksheets and other online materials go to *Teaching Short Films* at **www.bfi.org.uk/tfms** and enter User name: **shorts@bfi.org.uk** and Password: **te1203sf**.

Assessment

The fair assessment of group practice should not prove to be an obstacle in the practical production of short films. The assessment criteria for particular units should be made clear in the examination specifications for the course that you are teaching. These frequently leave teachers with some discretion in how to award marks for particular production tasks, however, it is essential that these be shared with all learners once an assessment methodology has been finalised by the course team. The assessment needs to account for learning in terms of knowledge, understanding and technical skills acquisition in both the production process and within the completed short film. An accompanying folder of the materials used within each production will help teachers to make fair assessments of individuals' input in the development of the short film.

Glossary

This glossary is also available as a downloadable photocopiable student resource.

Bridging shot
A shot that connects two shots from the same scene or to connect one scene to another by showing a change in time or location.

Cinematography
The art of positioning a camera and lighting a scene – the composition of the image with the camera and the light: 'painting moving images with light'.

Close-up
A picture that shows a fairly small part of the scene, such as a character's face, in great detail so that it fills the screen. It abstracts the subject from a context.

Codes
Commonly accepted and understood patterns or modes of representation in films.

Composition
The complete arrangement of a scene (by the director). The process includes camera angles, framing, lighting, properties, the layout of the scene and the movement of the camera.

Connotation
The implicit meaning of a word or phrase. In film connotation refers to the suggestive qualities of dialogue, sound, settings, images, et al.

Continuity (or invisible) editing
The editing style characteristic of the Hollywood system and classic narratives for the showing of cause and effect.

Conventions
Elements of plot, character, *mise en scène* and other aspects of film language associated with particular genres and styles.

Cropping
An important element of framing – cropping is the way in which the frame is used to exclude aspects of the *mise en scène*.

Crossing the line
Breaking the 180-degree rule of continuity editing.

Cross-cutting
Editing device – cutting back and forth between two locations or characters to suggest a relationship between them, eg that one is approaching the other.

Cutaway
A sudden change to another scene of action or angle.

Denotation
The literal meaning of a word or phrase in literature. In film the term applies to the process of describing images and sounds represented in films/other media texts.

Digital technologies
Refers to any system for recording and reading information – images, sounds – in computer-based numerical codes rather than in the older 'analogue' systems where information is directly stored on film or tape. Besides being easier to access, manipulate and store than analogue copies, digital versions of texts are all of equal quality.

Dissolve
An edit where one image gradually replaces the other.

Editing
The process by which shots are put together into sequences or scenes. Usually described according to rhythm or pace (ie the varying lengths of the shots in the sequence) and type of transition.

Establishing shot
A long shot, often the first in a sequence that sets up, or 'establishes', a scene's setting and/or its participants.

Flashback
A narrative device that allows the audience insights in to characters' past experiences or motivations.

Frame
Either the individual images that comprise a filmstrip or the rectangular shape of the recorded image.

Jump cut
Any cut that draws attention to itself.

Long shot
A shot that shows all or most of a fairly large subject (for example, a person) and usually much of the surroundings.

Match on action
A cut between two shots of the same action from different angles, but giving the impression of the continuity of action.

Medium shot
In such a shot the subject or actor and its setting occupy roughly equal areas in the frame.

Micro short
A short film of less than 90 seconds in length.

Mise en scène

Literally, 'put in the picture': the combined effect of all the visual elements in the frame. Includes location, set, props, costume, make-up and lighting.

Montage

A style of editing or 'mounting' images in such a sequence that new meanings arise from their juxtaposition.

Narrative

The events happening to characters within a story and told over time, in chronological order.

Objective shot

A shot that provides an audience with privileged knowledge, and which might not be available to the characters in the film.

Panning shot

A shot in which the camera moves on a horizontal plain, from left to right or vice versa.

Plot

The events in an individual narrative and how they are arranged.

Reaction shot

A close-up in which an actor is seen to respond to an action.

Rough cut

The rough cut contains the entire film in a continuous sequential order including the approximate running time to see how the film works.

Rushes (clips)

The unedited shots.

Shot/reverse shot

A film technique wherein one character is shown looking at another character, and then the other character is shown looking 'back' at the first character; frequently used in shooting conversations between characters.

Subjective (point-of-view) shot

A shot that shows what a character is looking at.

Take

The shot secured from the point of turning the camera on, to turning it off. Takes of each shot are generally numbered and the number of each successive take is increased until the filming of the shot is completed.

Tracking shot

The action of physically moving the camera along a track in order to follow an action or reveal a scene.

Treatment

A written representation of the film, used as an overview of the film prior to the finalisation of the shooting script.

Two-shot

The two-shot shows two people in the frame.

References and resources

Bibliography

K Adelman (2004) *The Ultimate Filmmaker's Guide to Short Films: Making it Big in Shorts,* Michael Wiese Productions

J Bell *Eat My Shorts*, Sight & Sound, May 2004

L Cowgill, (2005) *Writing Short Films: Structure and Content for Screenwriters*, 2nd ed, Lone Eagle

P Cooper and K Dancyger (1999) *Writing the Short Film*, 2nd ed, Focal

H Curtis, (2005) *Hillman Curtis on Creating Short Films for the Web*, New Riders

John Ellis (www.bfi.org.uk/features/freecinema/archive/ellis-freecinema.html)

E Elsey and A Kelly (2002) *In Short: A Guide to Short Film-making in the Digital Age*, BFI

S Field (2005) *Screenplay: The Foundations of Screenwriting*, Delta

P Fraser and B Oram (2003) *Teaching Digital Video Production*, BFI

T Harding (2001) *The Video Activist Handbook*, Pluto

R Harman, J Lawrence and J Walker (2003) *The Beginning Filmmaker's Guide to a Successful First Film*, Walker & Company

C Jones and G Jolliffe (2006) *The Guerilla Filmmaker's Handbook*, 3rd ed, Cassell Academic. This is a complete handbook for low-budget filmmaking in the UK. It includes a step-by-step guide from development to exhibition, with often amusing case studies from the authors' own low-budget work (including *Urban Ghost Story*); and a Film Producers Toolkit providing production templates, draft contracts and a facilities directory.

E Levy (1994) *Making a Winning Short: How to Write, Edit and Produce a Short Film*, Owl

F Levy (2004) *Short Films 101: How to Make a Short Film and Launch Your Filmmaking Career*, Perigree

I Lewis (2001) *How to Make Great Short Feature Films: The Making of Ghosthunter* [book and DVD], Focal

R McKee (1999) *Story: Substance, Structure, Style and The Principles of Screenwriting*, Regan Books

S Quy *Getting Your Short Film Shown*, Media Magazine, 11, February 2005

S Quy *In Short Supply*, Media Magazine, 11, February 2005

R Raskin, (2002) *The Art of the Short Fiction Film: A Shot by Shot Study of Nine Modern Classics*, McFarland

P Rea and D Irving (2000) *Producing and Directing the Short Film and Video*, 2nd ed, Focal

R Rodriguez (1995) *Rebel without a Crew: How a 23-Year-Old Film-maker with $7000 Became a Hollywood Player,* Dutton

S Sheridan (2004) *Developing Digital Short Films*, Pearson

C Thurlow (2005) *Making Short Films: The Complete Guide from Script to Screen*, Berg

Magazines

Res This American magazine focuses on innovation and experimentation in short film, music and the digital arts. Each issue (six per year) comes with a compilation DVD mounted on the cover and the annual compilation DVDs, *Best of Resfest*, are also a useful resource.

Showreel A quarterly magazine aimed at new filmmakers, students and film enthusiasts. Covering all aspects of filmmaking from concept to distribution. Contains entertaining and in-depth articles about techniques, equipment, news, events and awards, director and producer profiles, job descriptions, finance, training and education, written by professional journalists and filmmakers.

Sight & Sound Features informed commentary on world cinema. Extensive DVD coverage and every new cinema release reviewed with full synopses and credits. Occasional cover-mounts such as the *Digital Shorts* compilation are given away free to subscribers.

Vertigo Published quarterly (three print and one electronic issue). Champions innovation and diversity in form and culture for independent film and the moving image.

DVD compilations

See also pages 16 and 17.

Best of Resfest – Vol 1–3

Best v Best – Vol One (includes *Two Cars, One Night*)

Best v Best – Vol Two

Cinema 16 – British Short Films (includes *About a Girl*), Momac Films, 2003

Cinema 16 – European Short Films, Momac Films, 2004
Cinema 16 – American Short Films, Momac Films, 2006
Moving Shorts (includes *About a Girl*, *Two Cars, One Night* and 8 other
    award-winning short films), BFI, 2006 – for more information go to:
    www.bfi.org.uk/education/teaching/movingshorts/
Onedotzero DVDs – Vols 1–4
Raindance Film Festival Shorts – annual DVD
Screening Shorts, BFI, 2004 (www.bfi.org.uk/education/teaching/
    screeningshorts)
The Work of Director Spike Jonze, Directors Label Volume 1
The Work of Director Chris Cunningham, Directors Label Volume 2
The Work of Director Michel Gondry, Directors Label Volume 3

Filmography

About a Boy (Chris and Paul Weitz, UK, 2002)
About a Girl (Brian Percival, UK, 2001)
As I Was Falling (Rachel Tillotson, UK, 1999)
Bypass, The (Amit Kumar, UK, 2003)
Coffee and Cigarettes (Jim Jarmusch, USA, 2003)
Dad's Dead (Chris Shepherd, UK, 2002)
Delusions in Modern Primitivism (Daniel Loflin, USA, 2000)
Desserts (Jeff Stark, UK, 1998)
Divorcing Jack (David Caffrey, UK, 1998)
Endgame (Gary Wicks, UK, 2001)
Enemy at the Gates (Jean-Jacques Arnaud, DL/GB/IE/USA/FR, 2001)
Gasman (Lynne Ramsay, UK, 1997)
Ghosthunter (Simon Corris, UK, 2001)
Helicopter (Ari Gold, USA, 2000)
How They Got There (Spike Jonze with Mark Gonzales, USA, 1997)
How to be the Perfect Chav (Lucy Whiteside and Kellie Munckton, UK, 2006)
How to Submit Your Short Film to the Academy (extra feature on the 75th
Annual Academy Awards short films DVD)
Jack (Francis Ford Coppola, USA, 1996)
Jump (Simon Fellows, UK, 2001)
King Kong (Peter Jackson, New Zealand, 2005)
La Jetée (Chris Marker, FR, 1962)
Lay it Down (Michael Cargile, USA, 2001)
Le Cheval 2.1 (Stephen S Haywood and Kirk Kirkland, UK, 2005)
Light of Darkness, The (Michael Cargile, USA, 1998)
Living in Oblivion (Tom DiCillo, USA, 1995)
Lord of the Rings, The (Trilogy, Peter Jackson, New Zealand, 2001–3)

Lunch Date, The (Adam Davidson, USA, 1991)
Making It! As I was Falling at www.depict.org.uk
Making of Dad's Dead, The (on the Ondedotzero Volume 2 DVD)
Making of Ghosthunter, The (accompanies the *How to Make Great Short Feature Films* book)
My Wrongs #8245–8249 & 117 (Chris Morris, UK, 2002)
Non-Fat (Oliver Manzi, UK, 2004)
Once Were Warriors (Lee Tamahori, New Zealand, 1994)
Pitch, The (Doug Ellin, USA,1993)
Player, The (Robert Altman, USA, 1992)
Red Road (Andrea Arnold, UK, 2006)
Rubber Johnny (Chris Cunningham, UK, 2005)
Rumble Fish (Francis Ford Coppola, USA, 1983)
Scummy Man (Paul Fraser, UK, 2006)
Talking with Angels (Yousaf Ali Khan, UK, 2003)
Tama Tu (Taika Waititi, New Zealand, 2005)
Ten Minutes (Ben Mole, UK, 2002)
Two Cars, One Night (Taika Waititi, New Zealand, 2003)
Visions of Light (Arnold Glassman, USA, 1992)
Warrior, The (Asif Kapadia, UK/FR/DL, 2001)
Wasp (Andrea Arnold, UK, 2003)
Wayne's World (Penelope Spheeris, USA, 1992)
Whale Rider (Niko Caro, New Zealand, 2002)

Organisations

An increasing number of organisations and businesses are keen to support small film projects. These range from creative and community-based organisations to those with a particular agenda. All provide interesting data that can supplement and maintain the contemporary nature of schemes of work on short film.

Big Film Shorts Distribution Company (www.bigfilmshorts.com)
Blinkx TV (www.blinkx.tv)
British Academy of Film & Television (www.bafta.org)
BBC Film Network (www.bbc.co.uk/mobile/ents/filmnetwork)
BBC One-Minute Movies (www.bbc.co.uk/films/oneminutemovies)
British Council (www.britishcouncil.org)
British Film Institute (www.bfi.org.uk)
Cineclub (www.cineclub.org.uk)
Cinema 16 (www.cinema16.co.uk)
Curzon Cinemas (www.curzoncinemas.com)
Dazzle short film agency (www.dazzlefilms.co.uk)

Film Distributors Association
(www.launchingfilms.com/distribution/index.html)
Film 4 (www.channel4.com/film)
Film London (www.filmlondon.com)
Future Shorts (www.futureshorts.com)
London Film Academy (www.londonfilmacademy.com)
London Film School (www.lfs.org.uk)
The Metropolitan Film School (www.metfilmschool.co.uk)
National Film and Television School (www.nftsfilm-tv.ac.uk)
Netribution (www.netribution.co.uk/features/index.html)
New Producers' Alliance (www.npa.org.uk)
New York Film Academy (www.nyfa.com)
Screen Daily (www.screendaily.com)
Screenonline (www.screenonline.org.uk/tours/shortfilm)
The Script Factory (www.thescriptfactory.co.uk)
Shooting People (www.shootingpeople.org)
Short Film Bureau (www.shortfilmbureau.com)
Shorts International (www.shortsinternational.com)
Silver Films (www.silverfilms.co.uk)
Skillset (www.skillset.org)
Stellar Network (www.stellarnetwork.com)
Talent Circle (www.talentcircle.co.uk)
Tiscali (www.tiscali.co.uk/entertainment/film/shortfilms/raindance)
UK Film Council (www.ukfilmcouncil.org.uk)
UK Film Talk (www.ukfilmtalk.co.uk)
UK Screen (www.ukscreen.com/prods/film)
Underground Films (www.undergroundfilms.net)

Short film festivals

The following list is not intended to be definitive, since new film festivals are constantly appearing. An up-to-date directory of over 600 international film festivals can be found at www.britfilms.com/festivals.

Bang Short Film Festival (www.bangshortfilmfestival.com)
Belfast Film Festival (www.belfastfilmfestival.org)
Birds Eye View Women's Film Festival (www.birds-eye-view.co.uk)
Brief Encounters, Bristol (www.brief-encounters.org.uk)
Cinemagic Film Festival for Young People, Belfast (www.cinemagic.org.uk)
Commonwealth Film Festival (Manchester) Shorthouse strand
(www.commonwealthfilm.com)
Darklight Film Festival, Ireland (www.darklight.ie)
Edinburgh Film Festival (www.edfilmfest.org.uk)

Exposures, Manchester (www.exposuresfilmfestival.co.uk)
Ffresh Student Film Festival of Wales (www.ffresh.com)
Firecracker Showcase: London's Asian Film Festival (www.firecracker-showcase.com)
First Light (www.firstlightmovies.com)
Flatpack Film Festival, Birmingham (www.7inch.org)
Kinofilm, Manchester International Short Film Festival (www.kinofilm.org.uk)
Leeds International Film Festival (www.leedsfilm.com)
Lovebytes International Festival of Digital Art and Media, Sheffield (www.lovebytes.org.uk)
Mountain Film Festival (www.mountainfilm.co.uk)
Oddball Challenge (www.oddballchallenge.com)
Onedotzero (www.onedotzero.com)
Raindance (www.raindance.co.uk)
Showcomotion Young People's Film Festival, Sheffield. (www.showcomotion.org.uk)
Super Shorts (www.supershorts.org.uk)
Talent Circle Super Shorts Festival (www.supershorts.org.uk)
Times BFI London Film Festival, The (www.lff.org.uk)
UK Jewish Film Festival Shorts (www.ukjewishfilmfestival.org.uk)

Short film competitions

Cloud 9 Short Film Festival Competition (Frontier Airlines) (www.bigfilmshorts.com/acquisitions/about_cloud_9.htm)
Cobravision (www.cobrabeer.com/cobravision)
Co-operative Young Film Makers Competition (www.3bears.co.uk/festival)
Depict! (www.depict.org.uk)
Nokia Shorts (www.nokiashorts.co.uk)
O2 / mFlix Smallest Film Festival (www.mflix.com)
Short Circuit (www.mediamagazine.org.uk)
Turner Classic Shorts Competition (www.tcmonline.co.uk/microsites/classicshorts)

Websites

● Educational websites

www.filmcentre.co.uk
www.hurtwoodmedia.com
www.longroadmedia.com
www.screenonline.org.uk
www.ukstudentfilms.co.uk

- **Web cinemas**

Web screens have a tendency to come and go. For a current list go to:
www.hollywoodindustry.com/HTML/features/2000/5_00/shortfilms5_00.htm

Atom Films (www.atomfilms.com)
Channel 4 (http://www.channel4.com/film/shortsandclips/shorts.html)
Exposure (www.exposure.co.uk/eejit/movieonline)
Exposures Film Festival (www.exposuresfilmfestival.co.uk/?page=watch)
iFilm (www.ifilm.com)
It's All Electric (www.itsallelectric.com)
The New Venue (www.newvenue.com)
Short Film of the Week Blog (www.shortfilmoftheweek.blogspot.com)
Tank TV (www.tank.tv)
UK Student Films (www.ukstudentfilms.co.uk)

Acknowledgements

I would like to thank my colleagues, students and trainee teachers at Central School of Speech and Drama, University of London, for their support and encouragement in writing this guide.

Thanks also to Vivienne Clark, Wendy Earle and Caren Willig at the BFI for their enthusiasm for the project and understanding with deadlines.

I would like to dedicate this guide to my family for putting up with my absence/nonsense for so long in the research and writing phases of this guide.